HEART HEALTHY

COOKBOOK FOR

BEGINNERS 2023 EDITION

THE BEST GUIDE FOR HEART HEALTHY OF LOW-SODIUM, LOW-FAT RECIPES WITH 30-DAY MEAL PLAN

PATRICIA HART

TABLE OF CONTENTS

INTRODUCTION

Heart disease is a complicated condition affecting the heart and blood vessels. This term describes various heart conditions, such as heart attack, heart failure, coronary artery disease, and heart attack. Many factors can influence the development of heart diseases, such as genetics, lifestyle choices, and medical conditions.

There are many lifestyle changes that you can make to lower your risk of developing heart disease. Adopting a healthy lifestyle is one of the best lifestyle changes. Heart-healthy eating habits emphasize nutrient-rich foods and limit the consumption of saturated and trans fats, cholesterol, sodium, and cholesterol. These foods can lead to plaque buildup in the arteries, raising the risk of developing heart disease.

Healthy diets are rich in fruits, vegetables, and whole grains. These foods are rich in nutrients and supply the body with vital vitamins, minerals, antioxidants, and other nutrients. For example, fruits and vegetables are rich in fiber and antioxidants that can lower blood pressure, decrease inflammation, and increase cholesterol.

Foods high in sodium, saturated and trans fats, cholesterol, or other unhealthy substances should be avoided. These include processed, fried, red meat, and high-fat dairy foods. Trans and saturated fats can lead to plaque buildup in the arteries. Cholesterol can block arteries and increase your risk of developing heart disease. High blood pressure is a risk factor for heart disease.

Changing your diet can dramatically reduce your chance of developing heart disease. A heart-healthy diet will help to reduce plaque buildup in the arteries and decrease the risk of developing heart disease. You can improve your heart health by focusing on nutrient-rich foods like fruits, vegetables, whole grains, and lean proteins. Also, avoid foods high in cholesterol, saturated fats, trans fats, sodium, and cholesterol.

The Heart Healthy Cookbook for Beginners 2023 Edition will be an excellent resource for anyone who wants to improve their cardiovascular health. This book provides a complete guide to healthy eating and includes easy-to-follow recipe instructions and a 30-day meal plan. This cookbook will inspire you to create heart-healthy recipes, whether a novice or an experienced chef.

The book's first chapter explains the importance of eating a heart-healthy diet. This chapter describes the heart disease process and how lifestyle and diet can be crucial in preventing it. This chapter also provides an overview of the book's purpose and content, giving readers a general idea of what they can expect from the following chapters.

The chapter's first section focuses on heart disease and risk factors. This section explains how slow-growing heart disease can occur over time and how lifestyle factors like diet, exercise, and smoking influence its development. This section also explains the importance of knowing your risk factors, such as age, family history, medical conditions, and high blood pressure.

The second section of this chapter is about the importance of eating a healthy diet. This section explains the importance of a healthy diet and how it can reduce your risk of developing heart disease. This section discusses portion control, healthy food choices, and nutrition labels that help you identify low-sodium or low-fat foods.

The chapter's third section overviews the book and its purpose. This section explains how the book is intended to help readers create delicious and healthy meals that are low-fat, high in nutrients, and low in sodium. This section introduces the 30-day meal program, also included in the book. It provides readers with a week-by-week guide to healthy eating.

The Heart Healthy Cookbook for Beginners 2023 edition's first chapter provides a complete introduction to the importance and benefits of a healthy diet. This chapter explains the heart disease process and the lifestyle and diet factors that can help reduce its risk. This chapter also provides an overview of the book's purpose and content, giving readers a general idea of what they can expect from the next chapters. If readers read this chapter and follow the recommendations, they will be well on their path to bettering their heart health by eating right.

THE BASIC PRINCIPLES OF THE HEART-HEALTHY DIET

A heart-healthy diet refers to a diet that promotes heart health and lowers the risk of developing heart disease. Heart-healthy eating habits include a high intake of fruits, vegetables, whole grains, and lean proteins. They also limit saturated and trans fats, cholesterol, and sodium.

A heart-healthy diet includes nutrient-dense food as a critical component. Nutrient-dense foods are rich in vitamins, minerals, and essential nutrients and low in calories. Leafy greens, berries, nuts, whole grains, and lean proteins like fish, poultry, and legumes are all nutrient-dense foods.

A heart-healthy diet includes limiting the intake of saturated and trans fats, cholesterol, sodium, and other unhealthy foods. These foods can increase cholesterol, raise blood pressure and promote inflammation. Red meat, butter, and fried foods are rich in saturated and trans fats. Egg yolks and organ meats are high-cholesterol foods. Processed foods, canned soups, sauces, and fast food are all high in sodium.

Knowing the type and amount of fats consumed and what foods are allowed or not to be included in a heart-healthy diet is essential. Healthy fats such as avocado, fish, and nuts can lower cholesterol and decrease inflammation. Avoid trans fats. They are often found in processed foods and can increase your risk of developing heart disease.

A heart-healthy diet promotes good health and lowers the risk of developing heart disease. Individuals can improve their heart health by focusing on nutrient-dense foods and avoiding foods high in cholesterol, saturated fats, sodium, and cholesterol. They can also reduce their chance of developing heart disease.

IMPORTANT NUTRIENTS

A healthy diet provides essential nutrients to support heart health. This section provides an overview of the vital nutrients for a heart-healthy lifestyle. These nutrients include fiber, healthy fats, vitamins, and minerals.

Fiber

Fiber is a carbohydrate that the body does not absorb. Fiber passes through the digestive tract intact, adding bulk to stool and encouraging regular bowel movements. Fiber is essential for heart health as it can lower cholesterol levels by binding cholesterol in the digestive tract and preventing it from entering the bloodstream. Fiber is also critical for controlling blood sugar levels. Whole grains, fruits, vegetables, and legumes are all high in fiber, nuts, and seeds.

Healthy fats

Monounsaturated and multi-unsaturated healthy fats are good for your heart health. They can lower LDL (harmful) cholesterol levels. Omega-3 fatty acids, a type of healthy fat, have been shown to decrease inflammation and reduce the risk of developing heart disease. These fats can be found in salmon, tuna, nuts, seeds, and nuts. Avocado, olive oil, canola oil, and avocado are all good sources of healthy fats.

Vitamins

Vitamins and minerals are vital for maintaining a healthy heart. Vitamin C is an antioxidant that helps protect against heart disease. It reduces inflammation and prevents blood vessel damage. Vitamin C-rich foods include citrus fruits, dark leafy greens, and berries. Vitamin E, another antioxidant, can protect your heart. Nuts, seeds, and vegetable oil are all rich in vitamin E. Magnesium, a mineral that helps lower blood pressure and reduce the risk for heart disease, is an important one. Whole grains, nuts, and seeds are good sources of magnesium, as well as leafy greens, seeds, whole grains, and legumes.

These nutrients can be incorporated into a heart-healthy diet to reduce the risk of developing heart disease. The Heart Healthy Cookbook 2023 Edition offers delicious, nutritious recipes rich in fiber, healthy oils, vitamins, and minerals. This makes it easy to include these vital nutrients in your diet.

HOW DIFFERENT IS THE HEART-HEALTHY DIET FROM OTHER DIETS

There are many approaches to diets. Each one is unique and has its set guidelines. However, a heart-healthy diet differs from other diets in many vital ways.

One of the significant differences is the focus on nutrient-dense foods. Heart-healthy eating means eating foods rich in fiber, vitamins, minerals, and other essential nutrients. The diet should include fruits, vegetables, whole grains, and lean proteins. These foods are suitable for the heart and provide nutrients that help the body function at its best.

A heart-healthy diet differs from other diets in how they approach fats. Some diets emphasize cutting out all fats, while others focus on consuming healthy fats in moderation. Omega-3 fatty acids, found in nuts and fish, are vital for maintaining heart health and reducing inflammation.

Another area in which a heart-healthy diet is different from other diets is sodium. A high sodium intake can cause high blood pressure and increase your risk of developing heart disease. A heart-healthy diet reduces sodium intake by avoiding packaged and processed foods high in sodium and using herbs and spices instead to add flavor.

These are just a few differences between heart-healthy and other diets. A heart-healthy diet is also different in how it approaches portion control. While many diets focus on strict portion control to lose weight, a heart-healthy diet emphasizes portion management to keep your weight healthy and lower your risk of developing heart disease.

A heart-healthy diet emphasizes eating balanced meals, moderate amounts of healthy fats, low sodium intake, and portion control. It is a special diet that can be used to improve heart health and prevent heart disease.

PORTION CONTROL

A heart-healthy diet should include healthy portion control. Too much food can cause weight gain and other health issues. If we consume more calories than we burn, the body stores excess fat as fat. This can increase our risk of developing diabetes and heart disease.

Portion control is essential because our portion sizes have increased dramatically over the past 20 years. Studies have shown that people are now consuming more calories than ever before. This is due in large part to the increased portion sizes. Studies have shown that people eat more if given more significant portions regardless of hunger.

It is essential to control portion sizes by paying attention to serving sizes and being mindful of how much food we eat—using measuring cups or a scale to determine the appropriate dimensions. You can also use smaller cups, plates, and bowls to make the portions look more satisfying.

Avoiding calorie-dense foods such as fried foods and sugary drinks is also essential. These foods can be high in calories and low in nutrients, so you should limit their consumption.

A heart-healthy diet includes portion control. This can help you maintain healthy body weight, lower your risk of developing heart disease, and improve your overall health and well-being. You can have a healthy and satisfying diet that supports your heart health by being aware of portion sizes and choosing nutrient-dense foods.

BENEFITS OF A HEART-HEALTHY DIET

This chapter will discuss the many benefits of a healthy diet. A heart-healthy diet focuses on eating nutrient-dense foods, which promote good health and lower the risk of developing heart disease. We will be discussing the many benefits of a healthy diet. This includes lowering cholesterol, preventing heart disease, and improving overall health. We will also discuss foods especially beneficial to heart health, such as whole grains, fruits, and vegetables. You can improve your overall health by eating a heart-healthy diet and lowering your chances of developing chronic illnesses.

BENEFITS

A heart-healthy diet focuses on heart health. It restricts saturated fats, trans fats, cholesterol, and sodium and emphasizes fiber, vitamins, and mineral-rich foods. This diet has many benefits for your overall health and well-being.

- Heart disease risk reduced: A heart-healthy diet can lower your risk by reducing blood pressure, cholesterol levels, inflammation, and other risk factors. This diet encourages the consumption of whole grains, fruits, vegetables, lean proteins, and low levels of saturated and trans fats. These factors can lead to heart disease.

- Higher cholesterol levels: A heart-healthy lifestyle can improve cholesterol levels. It reduces the intake of saturated and trans fats. These fats raise "bad" cholesterol levels or low-density lipoprotein. This diet emphasizes fiber-rich foods like whole grains, which can lower LDL cholesterol.

- Lower blood pressure: A heart-healthy lifestyle can lower blood pressure. This is possible by decreasing sodium intake, which can lead to high blood pressure. This diet encourages the consumption of whole grains, fruits, vegetables, legumes, and lean proteins, which naturally have low sodium levels.

- Better weight management: A heart-healthy diet is an excellent way to lose weight. It encourages the consumption of healthy, nutrient-dense foods, low in calories, like fruits, vegetables, whole grains, and vegetables. This diet restricts the intake of high-calorie, high-fat foods that can lead to obesity and weight gain.

- Type 2 diabetes risk reduced: A heart-healthy diet can reduce your risk by encouraging the intake of whole grains and fiber-rich foods. This can help to regulate blood sugar levels. This diet restricts the intake of foods high in glucose, which can lead to rapid spikes.

- Improved digestion health: Fiber is a crucial ingredient in a heart-healthy diet. It promotes regular bowel movements and reduces the chance of constipation. A diet rich in fruits and vegetables is essential to support your digestive health.

- Better overall health: A heart-healthy diet can improve overall health by providing essential nutrients to the body vital for good health and preventing chronic diseases. This diet is rich in nutrients, such as whole grains, fruits, and lean proteins. These foods can supply the body with vitamins and minerals.

BENEFITS SPECIFIC FOODS

Discuss the health benefits of fruits, vegetables, and whole grains. These foods are especially good for your heart and should be part of a healthy diet.

Vegetables and fruits are rich in fiber, vitamins, and minerals and low in calories. They are high in antioxidants, essential for good health, and reduce the risk for chronic diseases like heart disease. The fiber in vegetables and fruits can lower cholesterol, regulate blood sugar and promote healthy digestion. Potassium, found in many vegetables and fruits, can also help to lower blood pressure. This is an essential factor in the prevention of heart disease.

Whole grains are an essential part of a healthy diet. Whole grains are high in fiber which can reduce cholesterol and regulate blood sugar. They also contain important nutrients like iron, B vitamins, and magnesium. Whole grains are a good carbohydrate source, providing a vital energy source for the body. Whole grains include whole grains such as brown rice, whole wheat bread, and quinoa.

Lean protein sources such as chicken and fish are essential for heart health. These foods are low-saturated fat and can help maintain muscle tissue. Omega-3 fatty acids are found in fatty fish like salmon and tuna. They can reduce inflammation and help lower the risk of heart disease.

A heart-healthy diet should limit foods high in saturated fats, trans fats, cholesterol, or sodium. These foods include processed foods, red meat, fried foods, and foods high in added sweetness. These foods can increase cholesterol and inflammation, leading

A heart-healthy diet should emphasize nutrient-dense foods like fruits, vegetables, and lean proteins. It must also limit saturated and trans fats, cholesterol, and sodium. These foods can help reduce your risk of developing heart disease. They also improve your overall health.

FOODS TO EAT, LIMIT, AND AVOID

This chapter will provide an overview of which foods should be limited or eliminated from a heart-healthy diet. A heart-healthy diet is low in saturated and trans fats and cholesterol and high in fiber, vitamins, and minerals. This chapter will discuss the importance of eating heart-healthy foods and the risks associated with eating foods high in unhealthy fats or sodium. We will also give guidance on how to read nutrition labels to make informed food choices that can help you keep your heart healthy and lower your risk for chronic diseases like diabetes and heart disease.

FOODS TO INCLUDE

A heart-healthy diet is rich in nutrients that provide the body with all the vitamins, minerals, fiber, and other essential nutrients required to function well. It also keeps the heart healthy. These are the foods you should include in a heart-healthy eating plan:

- Fruits: These fruits are rich in vitamins, minerals, and antioxidants that can reduce your risk of developing heart disease. Heart-healthy fruits include apples, citrus fruits, and pears, as well as bananas, bananas, and Kiwis.

- Vegetables: Another essential part of a healthy diet is vegetables. These vegetables are low in calories and high in fiber. They also contain vitamins and minerals. For heart health, leafy greens like spinach and kale, as cruciferous veggies such as broccoli, cauliflower, and other cruciferous vegetables, are particularly beneficial.

- Whole grains: Whole grains such as whole-wheat bread and brown rice are fiber-rich. This can lower cholesterol and help reduce the risk of developing heart disease.

- Lean protein sources: These lean protein sources include skinless poultry, fish, and legumes (beans and lentils) essential for maintaining muscle mass and providing the body with essential nutrients without adding too much-saturated fat.

- Low-fat dairy products: Low-fat dairy products such as yogurt, milk, and cheese are good sources of calcium and other essential nutrients without too much fat.

- Nuts & seeds: Nuts & seeds are good sources of healthy fats, fiber, and protein. Almonds, walnuts, and chia seeds are all excellent options for heart health.

These foods can be incorporated into your diet to help create a healthy eating plan for your heart.

FOODS TO AVOID

These foods contain a lot of saturated and trans fats, cholesterol, and sodium. This can increase your risk of developing heart disease and high blood pressure.

Here are some foods you should avoid or limit when following a heart-healthy diet:

- Processed meats: These processed meats, such as bacon, sausages, and deli meats, are high in sodium and saturated fats. These foods can raise cholesterol, blood pressure, and inflammation, and all this contributes to the development of heart diseases.
- Fried foods: Fried chicken, French fries, and onion rings are high-calorie and unhealthy. These foods can raise cholesterol, clog arteries and lead to obesity and weight gain, all of which are risk factors for developing heart disease.
- High-fat dairy products: Butter, cheese, whole milk, and other dairy products are high in saturated oil and cholesterol. This can increase your risk of developing heart disease. You can reduce unhealthy fat by switching to low-fat dairy products or fat-free milk products.
- Pre-packaged and processed foods: These foods, such as chips, cookies, cakes, and other snacks, are high in unhealthy fats, added sugars, sodium, and unhealthy cholesterol. These foods have little nutritional value and can lead to weight gain and other health issues.
- Sugary drinks: Sugary beverages such as soda, fruit juice, and sports drinks can be high in calories and add sugars. This can lead to weight gain, diabetes, and other health issues. You can reduce the sugar content of your diet by drinking water, herbal teas, and low-fat milk.
- Fast food: Burgers, fried chicken, and pizza are often high in unhealthy fats and sodium. Regular fast-food consumption can increase your risk of high blood pressure and heart disease.
- High-sodium foods: Foods high in sodium, such as pickles and canned soups, and pickles can raise blood pressure and lead to heart disease. You can lower your blood pressure by limiting sodium intake and using herbs and spices to flavor your food.

You can reduce your risk of developing heart disease by avoiding or limiting certain foods and instead focusing on whole, nutritious foods. The Heart Healthy Cookbook for Beginners 2023 edition offers a wealth of heart-healthy recipes to help you make healthier choices and improve your overall well-being

READING NUTRITIONAL LABELS

It is essential to be able to read nutrition labels and make informed food choices. This skill will help you maintain a healthy diet. In the "Heart Healthy Cookbook For Beginners 2023 edition," Chapter 4 explains how to read nutrition labels and provides the information readers need to make informed food choices.

A nutrition label is a panel that appears on food packaging and provides information about the nutritional content of the food. The nutrition label provides information about the food's serving size, serving sizes, calories per portion, and various nutrients like fat, sodium, and carbohydrates.

The serving size is one of the most important aspects of a nutrition label. Because all the nutritional information on a nutrition label is based on the listed serving size, this is crucial. You need to pay attention to the serving size to avoid eating too many calories and nutrients.

Nutrient content is another essential aspect to consider when reading nutrition labels. It is important to reduce saturated and trans fats, cholesterol, sodium, and other harmful substances in a heart-healthy diet. You can view the nutrition label to see how many nutrients are in each food item so you can make informed decisions about including it in your diet.

The nutrition label also provides information on the essential nutrients for heart health, including vitamins and minerals. You can make better choices and improve your overall health by looking for foods high in these nutrients.

The "Heart Healthy Cookbook for Beginners 2023 Edition" also offers guidance on how to read nutrition labels such as "low fat," "low sodium," and "organic." This will help readers decide what foods they eat and buy.

Understanding how nutrition labels are read is essential to maintaining a healthy diet. You can make informed choices about what you eat by looking at each food item's nutritional content and serving size. This will help you to improve your overall health.

TIPS FOR PREPARING HEART-HEALTHY MEALS

You don't need a complicated or tedious diet to eat a healthy, heart-healthy diet. You can make delicious meals that are good for your heart health by adjusting your cooking techniques and ingredients. This chapter will give you practical tips to prepare heart-healthy meals that taste great, are nutritious and are easy to make.

- Meal planning: By planning your meals, you can make better choices and avoid eating unhealthy or fast food. Choose heart-healthy recipes with whole grains, lean proteins, and fruits. To prevent food waste and money, make a grocery list. To make meal preparation easier and faster, you can prepare the ingredients ahead of time, such as washing and cutting vegetables.

- Cooking methods: How you cook your food can significantly affect its nutritional value. Choose heart-healthy cooking techniques such as roasting, baking, and steaming. Avoid deep-frying and frying as they can increase fat and calories. Choose healthier oils like avocado oil and olive oil when cooking.

- Flavorful substitutions are an essential part of a healthy diet. You can add flavor to your food using herbs, spices, or other delicious ingredients instead of salt and high-sodium seasonings. You can try fresh herbs such as rosemary, basil, garlic, and ginger to add some zest to your meals. You can substitute butter and vegetable oils with healthy fats such as avocado or olive oil.

- Portion control is essential for maintaining a healthy weight and avoiding overeating. You can control the amount of food you eat by using smaller plates and bowls. Half of your plate should be vegetables and fruits. One quarter should contain lean proteins, and the other should include whole grains. Do not eat second-sized portions, and listen to your body's signals of hunger and fullness.

- Your meal presentation is critical to enjoying your meals. Use a variety of colorful fruit and vegetable to make your meals more visually appealing. Healthy garnishes such as fresh herbs and sliced avocado can add flavor to your meals. Your meals will be more enjoyable if they are presented well. This can help you to stick to your healthy eating habits.

These tips will help you create heart-healthy meals. You should plan, use heart-healthy ingredients and cooking methods, limit portions, and visually make your meals attractive. You'll soon discover healthy eating is easy, tasty, and good for your heart.

Now that you have all the preparations let's start cooking!

BREAKFAST RECIPES

Oatmeal with Berries, Almond Milk Recipe

This oatmeal recipe is great for a healthy start to your day. It's packed with flavor and nutrients. Oats have a high fiber content that helps lower cholesterol. Berries are rich in antioxidants, vitamins, and other nutrients that can support heart health. Almond milk can be used as a dairy substitute. It has a creamy texture and a pleasant flavor and is low in cholesterol.

Ingredients:

- 1 cup steel-cut oatmeal
- 2 cups of water
- 1 cup unsweetened almond buttermilk
- 1/2 teaspoon cinnamon
- 1/2 tsp vanilla extract
- 1 cup mixed berries (strawberries, blueberries, raspberries)
- 1/4 cup chopped almonds
- 1 tbsp maple syrup or honey (optional).

Instructions:

- Place the steel-cut oatmeal, water, almond milk, and cinnamon in the bread machine.
- Choose the "porridge function" and set the timer to 30 minutes.
- While the oats cook, wash and chop the mixed fruits and set them aside.
- After the timer has elapsed, take the oatmeal out of the bread machine and divide it into two bowls.
- Add the chopped almonds and mixed berries to each bowl.
- If desired, drizzle honey or maple syrup over the top
- Enjoy a heart-healthy breakfast.

Avocado Toast and Egg Recipe

Avocado toast with eggs is a delicious and simple breakfast option packed with heart-healthy nutrients. Monounsaturated fats are found in creamy avocados. They can lower cholesterol and improve your heart health. This dish can be paired with a perfectly cooked egg for a nutritious and satisfying start to your day. This recipe is low in fat and sodium, making it an excellent choice for people who want a healthy diet.

Ingredients:

- 1 avocado ripe, pitted, and mashed
- 2 slices whole-grain bread
- 2 large eggs
- 1/2 tsp olive oil
- 1/4 teaspoon garlic powder
- 1/4 teaspoon black pepper
- 1/4 teaspoon sea salt

Instructions:

- Turn on the bread machine and heat it to whole-wheat mode.
- While the bread is heating up, mash your avocado in a small bowl. Add in the garlic powder and black pepper—season with sea salt. Mix thoroughly and place in a bowl.
- Mix the eggs in a small bowl.
- On medium heat, heat the olive oil in a nonstick skillet. Cook the eggs in the skillet for 2-3 minutes or until set. Season the eggs with salt and black pepper.
- Toast the bread in the bread maker until it is golden brown and crispy.
- Spread the mashed avocado mixture on each slice of bread once it is finished.
- Transfer the eggs onto the avocado toast slices using a spatula.
- If desired, sprinkle with sea salt and black pepper.
- Enjoy your heart-healthy breakfast immediately!

Greek Yogurt With Fruit and Nuts Recipe

Greek yogurt is rich in calcium and protein. It can be combined with fresh fruits and nuts to make a healthy and delicious breakfast. This recipe is quick to make and is excellent for anyone looking for a healthy and quick breakfast.

Ingredients:

- 1 cup plain Greek yogurt
- 1 cup mixed fruit (such as berries, sliced peaches, and kiwi).
- 1/4 cup chopped nuts (such as almonds or walnuts).
- 1 tablespoon honey

Instructions:

- Mix the honey and Greek yogurt in a bowl.
- Divide the mixture between two bowls.
- Each bowl should be topped with chopped nuts and mixed fresh fruits.
- Serve immediately

Heart-Healthy Breakfast Smoothie Recipe

This heart-healthy smoothie recipe will help you start your day off right. This smoothie contains nutritious ingredients and no added sugars or unhealthy fats. This smoothie is easy to prepare and can be modified to suit your tastes.

Ingredients:

- 1 ripe banana, peeled & sliced
- 1 cup frozen mixed berries
- 1 cup unsweetened almond buttermilk
- 1/2 cup plain Greek yogurt
- 1 tablespoon ground flaxseed
- 1 teaspoon honey (optional).

Instructions:

- Blend the banana, frozen mixed fruits, Greek yogurt, ground flaxseed, honey, and vanilla extract in a blender.
- Blend on high until smooth and creamy. You can add more almond milk if the mixture becomes too thick.
- Take the smoothie and pour it into a glass.

Veggie Omelette Recipe

This vegetable omelet recipe makes a delicious and healthy breakfast. It can also be modified with your favorite vegetables. This omelet recipe is low in fat and salt, making it an ideal choice for those who want a healthy diet.

Ingredients:

- 2 large eggs
- 2 tbsp skim milk
- 1/2 cup chopped vegetables (such as tomatoes, onions, peppers, and mushrooms),
- 1/4 teaspoon salt
- 1/4 teaspoon black pepper
- 1 tsp olive oil

Instructions:

- Heat a nonstick skillet on medium heat.
- Mix the eggs, skim milk, salt, and pepper in a small bowl.
- Heat 1 tablespoon olive oil in a skillet.
- Place the chopped vegetables in a skillet. Cook for 2 to 3 minutes or until softened.
- Let the eggs mix and cook on the vegetables for 2 to 3 minutes or until the top of the omelet is set.
- Flip the omelet carefully with a spatula. Continue cooking for another 1-2 minutes or until fully cooked.
- Place the omelet on a plate and heat it.

Whole Grain Pancakes With Fruit Recipe

Whole grain pancakes with fruits are delicious and healthy breakfast options. They are low in fat and salt, easy to make, and can be made using a bread maker. These pancakes are made with whole wheat flour, oats, and fresh fruits and will satisfy you all morning.

Ingredients:

- 1 cup whole wheat flour
- 1/2 cup rolled oatmeal
- 2 tablespoons brown sugar
- 1 teaspoon baking powder
- 1/2 teaspoon baking soda
- 1/4 teaspoon salt
- 1 egg
- 1 cup milk
- 1 tablespoon vegetable oil
- 1 teaspoon vanilla extract
- 1 cup fresh fruit (blueberries, strawberries, or sliced bananas).

Instructions:

- Combine the whole wheat flour, rolled oatmeal, brown sugar, baking powder, and baking soda in a large bowl.
- Mix the egg yolk, milk, vegetable oil, and vanilla extract separately.
- Mix the wet ingredients with the dry ingredients and stir to combine.
- Gently fold in the fruit.
- Turn on the bread machine to the "Dough" setting.
- Spray non-stick cooking spray on the bread machine griddle.
- Use a measuring cup or ladle to spoon the batter onto the griddle according to your preference.
- Turn off the bread machine and let it cool for about 3-5 minutes.
- With the remaining batter, repeat steps 7-8.
- Warm the pancakes with your favorite toppings, such as fresh fruit, honey, or Greek yogurt. Enjoy!

Healthy Breakfast Burrito

This hearty breakfast burrito has protein, fiber, and healthy fats and is an excellent choice for busy mornings. This is a great way to begin your day with a healthy and nutritious meal.

Ingredients:

- 1 cup whole wheat flour
- 1/2 cup all-purpose flour
- 1/2 teaspoon salt
- 1/2 teaspoon baking powder
- 1/2 teaspoon baking soda
- 1 tablespoon olive oil
- 1/2 cup warm water
- 1/2 cup black beans, drain and rinse
- 1/2 cup diced tomatoes
- 1/2 cup chopped onion
- 1/2 cup chopped bell pepper
- 4 large eggs
- 1/2 cup shredded reduced-fat cheddar cheese
- For garnish, fresh cilantro chopped

Instructions:

- Add the flour, salt, and baking powder to a bread machine pan. Choose the dough cycle, and the machine will do the rest.
- Once the dough is prepared, heat a large skillet on medium heat.
- Divide the dough into four equal pieces. Roll each piece into a ball. Roll each ball into thin tortilla shapes using a rolling pin or a floured surface.
- Each tortilla should be cooked in a skillet for approximately 1-2 minutes on each side until lightly browned and puffy.
- While the tortillas cook, heat the oil in a large skillet. Add the black beans, tomatoes, and onion to the skillet. Cook for about 5-7 minutes until the vegetables become soft.
- Mix the eggs in a bowl and add them to the skillet and the vegetables. Cook the eggs in a skillet until they are cooked.
- Divide the egg mixture and vegetable mixture equally between the tortillas. Sprinkle each tortilla with chopped cilantro and shredded cheese.
- Serve the burritos hot by rolling them up.

Quinoa Breakfast Bowl Recipe

This nutritious and delicious breakfast bowl is the best way to begin your day. This delicious and healthy breakfast bowl is packed with protein, fiber, and flavor and can be made easily using a bread maker.

Ingredients:

- 1 cup quinoa, rinsed
- 2 cups of water
- 1/4 cup unsweetened almond buttermilk
- 1/2 tsp vanilla extract
- 1/2 teaspoon ground cinnamon
- 1/2 cup fresh berries (such as blueberries, raspberries, or strawberries)
- 1/4 cup chopped nuts (such as almonds or walnuts).
- 1 tbsp maple syrup or honey (optional).

Instructions:

- Add the quinoa to the bread machine. Then, select the "cook" setting. Let the machine cook the quinoa till it becomes tender and fluffy.
- After the quinoa has been cooked, stir in the almond milk, vanilla extract, and ground cinnamon. Mix well.
- Divide the quinoa mixture between two bowls
- Each bowl should be topped with fresh berries or chopped nuts.
- If desired, drizzle honey or maple syrup over the top
- Serve immediately

Peanut Butter Banana Toast

This delicious, heart-healthy breakfast recipe is simple to prepare and fill. This recipe is low-fat and high in protein. It also contains fiber and healthy fats.

Ingredients:

- 1 ripe banana, mashed
- 2 slices whole grain bread
- 2 tablespoons natural peanut butter
- 1 tablespoon honey
- Cinnamon (optional).

Instructions:

- Start by mashing the ripe bananas in a bowl until they are smooth and creamy.
- Mix the honey and natural peanut butter in a bowl.
- Sprinkle some cinnamon over the mixture, and stir it in.
- Transfer the mixture evenly on the bread slices to the bread maker.
- Toast the bread in the bread maker for approximately 2-3 minutes or until it is crispy and golden brown.
- Take the bread out of the machine and cut it in half.
- Enjoy your heart-healthy peanut butter banana bread immediately.

Sweet Potato and Spinach Hash

This delicious sweet potato and spinach hash recipe make a nutritious, heart-healthy, easy, and delicious breakfast. This dish is low-salt in and high in saturated fats. It's also rich in fiber, vitamins, minerals, and other nutrients. This is an excellent way to start your day by enjoying a nutritious and filling meal.

Ingredients:

- 2 medium sweet potatoes, peeled then diced into small pieces
- 1 red bell pepper, chopped
- 1 onion, diced
- 2 cups fresh spinach chopped
- 1 teaspoon paprika
- 1 teaspoon dried thyme
- 1 teaspoon garlic powder
- 1/2 teaspoon black pepper
- 2 tablespoons olive oil

Instructions:

- Heat a nonstick skillet on medium heat. Heat olive oil until it shimmers.
- Cook the sweet potatoes in a saucepan for 5 minutes, stirring now and again.
- Cook the onion and diced red bell pepper in the skillet for 5 minutes. Stir occasionally.
- Stir in the chopped spinach and cook on medium heat until it is wilted.
- Mix in the paprika and thyme. Add garlic powder. Stir until combined.
- Cook the sweet potatoes and vegetables for 2-3 more minutes.
- Enjoy your delicious sweet potato-spinach hash hot.

LUNCH RECIPES

Sandwich with Turkey and Avocado

This sandwich is delicious, satisfying, and packed with heart-healthy ingredients such as turkey, avocado, and whole-grain bread. This sandwich is low in fat and sodium, making it an excellent choice for those who want a healthy diet.

Ingredients:

- 2 slices whole grain bread
- 3 oz. 3 oz.
- 1/4 avocado, sliced
- 1/4 cup arugula
- 1 tbsp. Honey mustard
- Salt and pepper are optional

Instructions:

- Toast two slices of whole-grain bread until they are lightly golden.
- Spread honey mustard onto one slice of the toasted bread.
- Serve the honey mustard with the sliced turkey breast.
- Toast some avocado with the turkey.
- Salt and pepper are optional.
- A few leaves of arugula can be added to the avocado.
- Add the second slice of toasted bread to the sandwich.
- Cut the sandwich in half and serve.

Grilled Chicken Salad with Veggies

This hearty salad is rich in protein, vitamins, and minerals, making it an excellent choice for a satisfying lunch. Grilled chicken is combined with fresh vegetables for a nutritious and delicious meal.

Ingredients:

- 2 breasts of boneless, skinless chicken
- 1 tablespoon olive oil
- 1/4 teaspoon black pepper
- 1/4 teaspoon garlic powder
- 1/4 teaspoon onion powder
- 4 cups mixed greens
- 1 medium cucumber, sliced
- 1 medium carrot, shredded
- 1/4 cup red onion, thinly chopped
- 1/4 cup cherry tomatoes, halved
- 1/4 cup balsamic vinegar vinaigrette
- Salt to taste (optional).

Instructions:

- Grill pan or grill pan on medium heat.
- Mix olive oil and black pepper in a small bowl.
- Use olive oil to brush the chicken breasts and season them with salt if desired.
- Grill the chicken on both sides for 6-8 minutes or until cooked.
- While the chicken cooks, wash and slice the cucumber and carrot. Slice the red onion and halves the cherry tomatoes.
- After the chicken has been cooked, take it off the grill and allow it to rest for a while.
- Combine the mixed greens with cucumber, carrot, red onions, cherry tomatoes, and carrot in a large bowl.
- Add the breasts of chicken to the bowl by dicing them.
- Toss the salad in the balsamic vinegar dressing and coat it.
- Enjoy your heart-healthy, delicious grilled chicken salad with vegetables immediately!

Quinoa, Lentil Salad with Roasted Vegetables

This nutritious and filling lunch idea is quinoa and lentil salad with roasted vegetables. This salad contains protein, fiber, vitamins, and other nutrients. It will keep you full for hours. It's rich in flavor thanks to the roasted vegetables, and the quinoa, lentils, and quinoa make it a satisfying and hearty meal.

Ingredients:

- 1 cup quinoa
- 1/2 cup green lentils or brown lentils
- 3 cups mixed vegetables (such as cherry tomatoes, bell peppers, and zucchini), chopped into bite-sized pieces
- 2 tablespoons olive oils
- 1 teaspoon dried oregano
- 1 teaspoon garlic powder
- Salt and pepper to taste
- 1 cup chopped fresh parsley leaves
- 1/4 cup feta cheese (optional)

Instructions:

- Preheat the oven to 400°F (200°C).
- Under cold running water, rinse the quinoa or lentils.
- Combine the quinoa, lentils, and 3 cups water in a large saucepan. Bring to a boil. Then reduce heat and simmer for approximately 20-25 minutes or until the quinoa is tender.
- Place the chopped vegetables on parchment paper lined baking sheets while the quinoa or lentils are heating up.
- Olive oil can be used to drizzle the vegetables. Mix to coat.
- Bake the vegetables for 20-25 minutes or until tender.
- After the lentils and quinoa have been cooked, drain the excess water and transfer them to a large bowl.
- Toss the roasted vegetables into the bowl.
- If necessary, season with salt and pepper.
- Optional: Sprinkle the salad with chopped fresh parsley and crumbled feta cheese.
- Serve immediately or keep in the refrigerator for up to three days.

Tuna Salad Lettuce Wraps

Tuna Salad Lettuce wraps are light and refreshing, and packed with flavor. This recipe substitutes high-fat mayonnaise with Greek yogurt, making it healthier than traditional tuna salad.

Ingredients:

- 2 cans tuna (in water and drained).
- 1/4 cup plain Greek yogurt
- 1/4 cup chopped celery
- 1/4 cup chopped red onion
- 1 tablespoon Dijon mustard
- 1 tablespoon of lemon juice
- 1 teaspoon garlic powder
- Salt and pepper to your liking
- Butter lettuce leaves for wrapping

Instructions:

- Combine the tuna, Greek yogurt, and diced celery in a bowl.
- To taste, add Dijon mustard, lemon juice, and garlic powder. Combine all ingredients in a bowl.
- Butter lettuce leaves should be washed and dried. Place the tuna salad in the middle of each leaf.
- To make a wrap, fold the bottom half of the lettuce leaf in half.
- You can eat it immediately or keep it in the refrigerator for up to two days.

Vegetable Wrap and Greek Yogurt

This Greek Yogurt and Vegetable Wrap makes a great lunch. This wrap is made with fresh vegetables, creamy Greek yogurt, and a hint of tangy Feta cheese. It's healthy and filling and easy to make.

Ingredients:

- 1 large whole-wheat tortilla
- 1/4 cup plain Greek yogurt
- 1/4 cup chopped cucumber
- 1/4 cup chopped tomato
- 1/4 cup chopped bell pepper
- 2 tablespoons crumbled Feta cheese
- 1/4 teaspoon black pepper
- 1/4 teaspoon dried oregano
- 1/4 teaspoon garlic powder

Instructions:

- Mix the Greek yogurt, black olive, dried oregano, and garlic powder in a small bowl.
- Spread the yogurt mixture on the tortilla. Leave a 1-inch border around the edges.
- Sprinkle the tomato, bell pepper, and chopped cucumber over the yogurt mixture.
- Sprinkle with crumbled Feta cheese.
- You can roll the tortilla tight, keeping the sides in check.
- Serve the wrap by cutting it in half.

Smoked Salmon Sandwich

A delicious, refreshing sandwich with smoked salmon and cucumber is great for light lunches or snacks. The sandwich is simple to make and has very low fat and salt, making it an excellent choice for people trying to eat healthily.

Ingredients:

- 4 slices whole grain bread
- 4 oz smoked salmon
- 1 small cucumber, thinly chopped
- 2 tablespoons low-fat cream cheese
- 1 tablespoon fresh dill chopped
- 1 tablespoon lemon juice
- To taste, grind black pepper

Instructions:

- Toast the whole-grain bread slices until they turn a light golden brown. Toast the bread using a toaster oven, grill, or oven. Put the toast aside.
- Mix the low-fat cream cheese with fresh dill, lemon zest, and ground black pepper in a small bowl to make a spread.
- Spread the cream cheese mixture on each slice of toast.
- Layer a thin layer of cucumber slices on top of the cream cheese mix.
- Sprinkle smoked salmon over the cucumber slices.
- Add another layer of cucumber slices to top of the smoked salmon.
- Add a few grinds of black pepper to the top of your sandwich.
- Close the sandwich by removing the last slice of toast.
- Split the sandwich in half diagonally
- Enjoy your delicious smoked salmon sandwich with cucumber.

Black Bean, Vegetable Quesadilla

Black Bean and Vegetable Quesadilla, a Mexican-inspired dish, is delicious and healthy. It's great for lunch and dinner. This is a great recipe to include vegetables in your diet while still enjoying the bold flavors of Mexican food. Here's how it is done:

Ingredients:

- 1 can black beans, drain and rinse.
- 1 red bell pepper, sliced
- 1 green bell pepper, sliced
- 1 onion, cut
- 1 clove minced garlic
- 1 teaspoon chili powder
- 1 teaspoon ground cumin
- 1 teaspoon paprika
- 1/2 teaspoon salt (optional).
- 1/4 teaspoon black pepper
- 4 whole wheat tortillas
- 1/2 cup shredded low-fat cheddar cheese
- 1 tablespoon olive oil

Instructions:

- Olive oil, garlic, onions, and peppers will be added to a large skillet on medium heat. Let vegetables cook for about 5-7 minutes or until tender.
- In a skillet, add black beans, cumin powder, cumin, and paprika. Stir together and continue cooking for 5 minutes until beans are hot and vegetables are tender.
- Heat a nonstick skillet on medium heat. Put one tortilla in the skillet. Add a quarter of your vegetable mixture to the tortilla. Sprinkle with cheese. To make a quesadilla, place another tortilla on top.
- Cook the tortillas for 2 to 3 minutes, until the cheese melts and the bottom, is golden brown. Then flip the quesadilla over and cook for another 2-3 minutes. Continue with the remaining tortillas and filling.
- Each quesadilla should be cut into four pieces and served immediately

Grilled Chicken & Veggie Skewers

Grilled Chicken and Veggie Skewers make a healthy and delicious meal that can be enjoyed at any time of year. This is a fun and easy way to enjoy fresh vegetables and protein, and it's great for people who want a low-fat or low-salt meal. Here is a quick recipe for Grilled Chicken & Veggie Skewers you can make at home:

Ingredients:

- 1 lb. boneless, skinless chicken breasts cut into 1-inch cubes
- 1 red bell pepper, seeds and cut into 1-inch pieces
- 1 green bell pepper, seeds and cut into 1-inch pieces
- 1 yellow onion cut into 1-inch pieces
- 1 zucchini cut into 1-inch pieces
- 1 tablespoon olive oil
- 1 tablespoon of lemon juice
- 1 teaspoon garlic powder
- 1 teaspoon dried oregano
- Salt and pepper to your liking

Instructions:

- Pre-heat your grill to medium heat
- Mix the olive oil with lemon juice, garlic powder, and oregano in a small bowl. Season with salt and pepper as needed.
- Place the vegetables and chicken on skewers and alternate between the vegetables and the chicken.
- Use the olive oil and herb mix to brush the skewers.
- Place the skewers on the barbecue and cook for 10-12 minutes or until the chicken and vegetables are cooked.
- Enjoy hot!

Chickpea Salad With Lemon and Parsley

Chickpea Salad With Lemon and Parsley is delicious and healthy. It's quick and easy to prepare and can be enjoyed anytime. This salad is a good choice for light lunches or as a side dish. It's full of protein, fiber, and flavor. Here are the steps to make it.

Ingredients:

- 2 cans chickpeas, drain, and rinse.
- 1/2 Red onion, chopped finely
- 1 red bell pepper, chopped
- 1/2 cup chopped fresh parsley
- 1/4 cup extra-virgin Olive Oil
- 2 tablespoons freshly squeezed lime juice
- 1/2 teaspoon salt
- Freshly ground black pepper, to your liking

Instructions:

- Mix the chickpeas with red onion, bell pepper, bell pepper, and chopped Parsley in a large bowl.
- Mix the olive oil with lemon juice, salt, and black pepper in a small bowl until well combined.
- Toss the dressing over the chickpea mix and coat.
- Wrap the bowl in plastic wrap and let it cool for 30 minutes. This will allow the flavors to blend.
- Give the salad a quick stir to distribute the dressing. Sprinkle some chopped parsley on top to add a new burst of flavor.

Whole Wheat Pita With Hummus and Veggies

Whole Wheat Pita with Hummus, Veggies is a healthy and delicious meal that's quick and easy to prepare. Pita bread, a Middle Eastern flatbread, is made with whole wheat flour. It's delicious with hummus, fresh vegetables, and other nutritious ingredients. This recipe is low in fat and salt, making it an excellent choice for people who want a healthy diet.

Ingredients:

- 4 pitas made from whole wheat
- 1 cup hummus
- 1 cup mixed vegetables (such as red bell peppers, cherry tomatoes, sliced cucumbers, and shredded carrots).
- 1 tablespoon olive oil
- 1 teaspoon lemon juice
- 1/4 teaspoon garlic powder
- Salt and pepper to taste

Instructions:

- Preheat your oven to 350°F (175°C). Bake the pitas for about 5-7 minutes or until they become slightly crispy.
- While the pitas bake, make the hummus. In a food processor, blender, or in food processor, blend the chickpeas with olive oil, lemon juice, and garlic powder. Blend until smooth.
- After the pitas have been baked, cool them out of the oven. Next, split each pita in half. Then open the pocket.
- Place 1/4 cup of hummus in the pita half and fill the pockets with the creamy spread.
- Each pita pocket should be filled with a handful of mixed vegetables. Divide them equally among the four pitas.
- Sprinkle olive oil on top of each pita and season it with salt and pepper.
- Enjoy your Whole Wheat Pita with Hummus, Veggies, and deliciousness immediately.

Goat Cheese and Roasted Red Pepper Sandwich

The Roasted Red Pepper and Goat Cheese Sandwich is a great lunch or dinner sandwich. This sandwich is full of flavor. It features sweet roasted red peppers and tangy goat cheese. This recipe will make this delicious sandwich.

Ingredients:

- 4 slices whole-grain bread
- 1 roasted red pepper, sliced
- 2 oz goat cheese
- 2 cups fresh baby spinach
- 2 tsp olive oil
- 1/4 teaspoon black pepper
- 1/8 tsp salt (optional)

Instructions:

- Start by roasting the red bell pepper. Preheat the oven to 425°F (218°C). The stem and seeds can be removed from the red pepper by cutting it in half. Place the skin-side down on a baking sheet. Bake for 20-25 minutes or until the skin is blackened and blistered.
- Transfer the peppers out of the oven to a bowl. Let the peppers cool in the bowl for 10-15 minutes before covering them with plastic wrap.
- Take the skin off the peppers and cut them into thin strips.
- Place the goat cheese on one side of each bread piece.
- Split the spinach between two slices of bread and top it with the roasted red pepper slices.
- Sprinkle the olive oil on top of the roasted red bell pepper slices. If desired, add black pepper and salt.
- Close the sandwich by putting the goat cheese side up.
- Slice the sandwiches in half, and serve immediately

Grilled Portobello Mushroom Sandwich

The grilled Portobello Mushroom sandwich is a healthy and delicious vegetarian sandwich. It is quick, easy to prepare, and great for lunch or dinner. This low-fat and salty recipe makes it an excellent choice for people trying to live a healthy lifestyle.

Ingredients:

- 4 large Portobello mushrooms, stems removed
- 2 tablespoons balsamic Vinegar
- 1 tablespoon olive oil
- 1 clove minced garlic
- 1/4 teaspoon black pepper
- 4 slices whole grain bread
- 1/4 cup hummus
- 1 small red onion, cut
- 1 small tomato, sliced
- 1/4 cup arugula

Instructions:

- Grill pan or grill pan on medium heat.
- Mix the balsamic vinegar and olive oil in a small bowl. Add the garlic, black pepper, and olive oil.
- Use the balsamic mix to brush the Portobello mushrooms, ensuring they are evenly coated.
- Place the mushrooms, gill-side down, on a grill pan or grid iron, and cook for 5-7 mins or until tender.
- Toast the whole grain bread slices while the mushrooms cook.
- Each slice of bread should be coated with 1 tablespoon of hummus
- Add the grilled mushrooms, red onion, tomato, and arugula to the bread.
- Serve immediately and enjoy

Sweet Potato Chili

Sweet Potato and black bean chili is a delicious vegan dish for a casual dinner or weekend meal. This recipe is rich in nutrients like sweet potatoes and black beans. It also has various spices that give it a strong and zesty taste.

Ingredients:

- 1 tablespoon olive oil
- 1 onion chopped
- 2 cloves of garlic, minced
- 2 teaspoons chili powder
- 1 teaspoon ground cumin
- 1/2 teaspoon smoked paprika
- 1/4 teaspoon cayenne pepper
- 2 medium sweet potatoes, peeled & diced
- 1 can (14.5 ounces) diced tomatoes, undrained
- 1 can (15 ounces) of black beans, rinsed.
- 1 cup water
- Salt to your taste (optional).
- Fresh cilantro, chopped (optional).

Instructions:

- Over medium heat, heat the olive oil in a large saucepan or Dutch oven. Cook the onion and garlic for 5 minutes.
- Stir in the cumin, chili powder, smoked paprika, and cayenne pepper. Stirring constantly for 1 minute until spices become fragrant.
- Add the sweet potatoes and diced tomatoes (with all their juices), black beans, and water to a large pot. Mix well.
- Bring the chili to a boil. Then reduce heat and simmer covered for 30-35 minutes or until sweet potatoes are tender.
- Salt the chili to taste.
- If desired, serve the chili hot with fresh cilantro garnish.

Broccoli, Cheddar Soup

Broccoli and Cheddar soup is comforting and classic for cold days. It's easy to prepare, delicious, nutritious, and straightforward. This recipe will teach you how to make a low-sodium, healthy version of broccoli and cheddar soup.

Ingredients:

- 2 Tbsp unsalted butter
- 1 medium onion chopped
- 3 minced garlic cloves
- 1/4 cup all-purpose flour
- 4 cups low-sodium vegetable broth
- 4 cups chopped broccoli florets
- 2 cups shredded low-fat cheddar cheese
- 1/2 cup plain Greek yogurt
- 1/4 teaspoon black pepper
- Salt to taste (optional).

Instructions:

- Melt the butter in a large saucepan over medium heat.
- Cook the minced garlic and chopped onion for 5 minutes.
- Mix the all-purpose flour with the garlic and onion. Stir to combine.
- Cook another 2-3 minutes, stirring continuously.
- Slowly add the low-sodium vegetable soup, stirring continuously to avoid lumps.
- Bring the soup to boil with the chopped broccoli florets.
- Reduce heat to low and cover the pot. Let the soup simmer for 15-20 minutes or until the broccoli becomes tender.
- Use an immersion blender to blend the soup until smooth.
- Bring the pot back to heat. Add the plain Greek yogurt and shredded low-fat cheddar cheese.
- Stir until cheese is melted and yogurt is fully incorporated.
- Salt the soup to your liking.
- If desired, serve the soup hot with extra shredded cheddar cheese or chopped broccoli florets.

Lentil Soup With Spinach

Lentil soup with spinach is a nutritious and healthy dish for cold winter days. This hearty soup is simple to make and rich in protein and fiber. It's an excellent choice for vegans and vegetarians. This recipe will teach you how to make a healthy and delicious Lentil Soup with Spinach. It is low in fat and salt.

Ingredients:

- 1 cup dried lentils, rinsed well and drained
- 1 large onion chopped
- 3 minced garlic cloves
- 1 teaspoon cumin
- 1 teaspoon coriander
- 1/2 teaspoon smoked paprika
- 4 cups low-sodium vegetable broth
- 2 cups baby spinach leaves
- 1 tablespoon olive oil
- Salt and black pepper are good for flavor

Instructions:

- Heat the olive oil in a large saucepan on medium heat. Stir in the chopped onion, and cook for about five minutes.
- Sauté the garlic, cumin, and coriander in a pot for 2-3 minutes.
- Add the rinsed, drained lentils and the low-sodium vegetable stock to the pot. Bring the mixture to a boil. Then reduce heat to low, and simmer the mixture for 25-30 minutes or until the lentils become tender.
- Stir the baby spinach leaves into the pot until they are wilted.
- Blend the soup with an immersion blender until smooth. Transfer the soup to an immersion blender, blend until smooth, and then return it to your pot.
- Season the soup with black pepper and salt to taste. You can start with some salt and then add more as needed. Keep in mind that low-sodium vegetable broth already has some salt.
- The Lentil Soup With Spinach can be served hot with extra baby spinach leaves or sprinkles of smoked paprika.

Grilled Vegetables and Feta Wrap

The Grilled Vegetable & Feta Wrap is quick, delicious, and perfect for lunch or dinner. This recipe is packed with nutrients and includes savory feta cheese. It's an excellent choice for vegetarians or anyone who wants a low-fat, low-salt meal.

Ingredients:

- 1 red bell pepper, sliced
- 1 zucchini, sliced lengthwise
- 1 yellow squash, cut lengthwise
- 1 red onion, cut
- 1 tablespoon olive oil
- 1/4 teaspoon black pepper
- 1/4 teaspoon garlic powder
- 1/4 teaspoon dried oregano
- 1/4 teaspoon paprika
- 4 whole wheat tortillas
- 1/2 cup crumbled Feta cheese
- 2 cups mixed greens

Instructions:

- Grill or pan on medium heat.
- Mix the red bell pepper, yellow squash, red onion, and garlic powder in a large bowl. Toss until coated.
- Grill the vegetables for 4-5 minutes per side or until tender and lightly charred.
- Take the vegetables off the grill and place them on a plate.
- For a few seconds, heat the whole wheat tortillas on a skillet or in the microwave for each side.
- Divide the grilled vegetables equally among the tortillas.
- Sprinkle crumbled Feta cheese over the vegetables.
- Each wrap can be made with a few mixed greens.
- Wrap the wraps tightly, and then serve.
- Enjoy your healthy Grilled Vegetable & Feta Wrap

Shrimp and Vegetable Stew

Shrimp and vegetable stir-fry are a delicious and healthy recipe for a quick weeknight dinner. This dish combines colorful shrimp with savory spices for a delicious and healthy meal.

Ingredients:

- 1 lb. large shrimp, deveined and peeled
- 1 red bell pepper, sliced
- 1 green bell pepper, sliced
- 1 yellow onion, cut
- 2 cloves garlic, minced
- 1 tablespoon grated ginger
- 1 tablespoon low-sodium soybean sauce
- 1 tablespoon cornstarch
- 2 tablespoons vegetable oils
- 1/4 teaspoon black pepper
- Chop scallions can be used as a garnish

Instructions:

- Mix the soy sauce and cornstarch in a small bowl. Add the black pepper. Set aside.
- Over high heat, heat the vegetable oil in a large saucepan or wok.
- Stir fry the ginger and garlic in a skillet for 30 seconds or until fragrant
- Stir fry the red bell pepper, green bell pepper, and sliced onion in a skillet for 2 to 3 minutes or until the vegetables soften.
- Stir fry the shrimp in the skillet for 2 to 3 minutes or until they turn pink.
- Stir fry the vegetables and shrimp for 1-2 minutes or until the soy sauce is thickened.
- Serve with chopped scallions (optional).

Baked Salmon and Asparagus

Baked salmon and asparagus are healthy and delicious dishes for a quick weeknight meal. The recipe is simple to prepare and requires only a few ingredients. Salmon is an excellent source of protein and omega-3 fatty acids, as well as vitamin D. Asparagus, is rich in fiber, vitamins, and minerals, and is a good source of both.

Ingredients:

- 4 (4 oz.) salmon fillets
- 1 lb asparagus, trimmed
- 2 tbsp olive oil
- 1 tsp lemon zest
- 1/2 teaspoon garlic powder
- 1/2 teaspoon paprika
- 1/4 teaspoon black pepper
- 1/4 tsp salt (optional)

Instructions:

- Preheat the oven to 400°F (200°C).
- Place parchment paper on a baking sheet.
- Season the salmon fillets with lemon zest, garlic powder, and paprika.
- Use 1 tablespoon olive oil to drizzle the salmon.
- Place the asparagus trimmed around the salmon fillets.
- Use the remaining 1 tablespoon of olive oil to drizzle the asparagus.
- Sprinkle some salt and black pepper on the asparagus.
- Bake the baking sheet for 12-15 minutes or until the salmon and asparagus are tender.
- Serve the salmon baked with the asparagus roasted on the side.

Grilled Chicken & Veggie Salad with Balsamic dressing

Grilled Chicken and Veggie Salad with Balsamic Dressing are a satisfying and healthy meal that can be enjoyed anytime. This meal is high in protein, fiber, and vitamins, making it an excellent choice for people who want to eat healthy but not sacrifice flavor.

Ingredients:

- 2 breasts of boneless, skinless chicken
- 1 large red bell pepper, cut into strips
- 1 large yellow bell pepper, cut into strips
- 1 medium zucchini, sliced into rounds
- 1 medium yellow squash, cut into rounds
- 1/2 red onion, cut
- 2 cups mixed greens
- 1/4 cup balsamic vinegar
- 2 tablespoons olive oils
- 1 teaspoon honey
- 1 clove garlic, minced
- Salt and pepper to your liking

Instructions:

- Pre-heat the grill to medium heat
- Season the breasts of chicken with salt and pepper according to your taste.
- Grill the breasts of the chicken for 5-6 minutes or until cooked through. Allow cooling.
- Mix the balsamic vinegar with olive oil, honey, and minced garlic in a large bowl. Season with salt and pepper as needed.
- Toss the red and yellow bell peppers, zucchini, and yellow squash in a bowl with the dressing.
- Grill the vegetables for 2-3 minutes per side or until tender and lightly charred. Allow to cool.
- Cut the chicken breasts into strips.
- Arrange the mixed greens, grilled veggies, and chicken strips in a large bowl.
- Serve immediately with any remaining dressing.

Brown Rice and Vegetable Bowl

Brown Rice and Vegetable Bowl are delicious and healthy recipes for quick and easy meals. This is an excellent way to include a variety of vegetables in your diet while still enjoying a delightful meal. This low-fat and salty recipe makes it an ideal choice for people trying to reduce their sodium intake.

Ingredients:

- 1 cup brown rice
- 2 cups of water
- 1 tablespoon olive oil
- 1 small onion chopped
- 2 cloves of garlic, minced
- 2 carrots, peeled & chopped
- 1 chopped red bell pepper
- 1 cup broccoli florets
- 1 cup chopped mushrooms
- 1 tablespoon low-sodium soybean sauce
- 1/2 teaspoon ground black pepper
- 1/2 teaspoon paprika
- 1 teaspoon garlic powder
- 1/4 teaspoon salt (optional)

Instructions:

- Rinse the brown rice in cold water. Drain. Combine the rice with 2 cups of water in a medium saucepan. Bring to a boil. Reduce heat to low and cover the pan. Let the rice simmer for 30 minutes or until all the water is absorbed.
- Heat the olive oil in a large skillet on medium heat while the rice cooks. Stir in the garlic and onion, and cook for 2-3 minutes.
- Cook the chopped carrots for 3-4 minutes or until they soften.
- Add the red bell pepper, chopped broccoli florets, and sliced mushrooms. Stirring occasionally, cook for about 5-7 minutes until vegetables are tender.
- Mix in the low-sodium soy sauce, black pepper, garlic powder, and salt (if desired). Mix well.
- Serve the vegetable mixture on top of the brown rice. You can season the mixture with chopped fresh herbs and nutritional yeast.

Red Pepper and Eggplant Sandwich

This delicious, healthy sandwich is great for lunch and dinner. This sandwich is full of flavor and nutrition and an excellent way to get your daily vegetable intake. This delicious sandwich recipe is here.

Ingredients:

- 1 medium-sized eggplant, cut into 1/2-inch thick rounds
- 1 red bell pepper, cut into strips
- 1/2 of red onion, cut
- 2 cloves minced garlic
- 2 tablespoons olive oil
- 1/4 teaspoon black pepper
- 1/4 teaspoon salt (optional).
- 4 whole wheat sandwich buns
- 1/2 cup hummus
- 1/4 cup fresh parsley leaves

Instructions:

- Preheat the oven to 400°F (200°C).
- Place the eggplant slices in one layer on a baking tray. Sprinkle with 1 tablespoon of olive oil. Bake for between 20-25 minutes or until eggplant is tender.
- Heat 1 tablespoon olive oil in a large skillet on medium heat. Cook the red bell peppers and red onions for about 5-7 minutes or until tender and lightly browned. Cook for another 1-2 minutes.
- Spread 2 tablespoons of hummus onto each sandwich bun's bottom half to assemble the sandwiches. A few slices of roasted eggplant, along with a generous amount of red pepper and onion mix, are all you need to top your sandwich. Add fresh parsley leaves.
- Serve immediately and enjoy

Spinach and Feta Omelette

Spinach and Feta Omelette is a delicious and nutritious breakfast or brunch option that is easy to prepare and packed with flavor. This recipe is perfect for those who want a quick, healthy, and satisfying meal to start their day. The combination of spinach and feta cheese provides a good balance of protein and vegetables, while the eggs add a rich and fluffy texture.

Ingredients:

- 2 large eggs
- 1/4 cup chopped spinach
- 1/4 cup crumbled feta cheese
- 1 tablespoon olive oil
- 1/4 teaspoon black pepper
- Pinch of salt (optional)

Instructions:

- In a mixing bowl, beat the eggs with the black pepper and a pinch of salt (if used) until they are well combined and frothy.
- Heat the olive oil in a non-stick frying pan over medium heat.
- Add the chopped spinach to the pan and sauté for 1-2 minutes until it starts to wilt.
- Pour the beaten eggs over the spinach in the pan and cook for 2-3 minutes until the edges of the omelet begin to set.
- Use a spatula to lift the edges of the omelet and let the uncooked eggs flow underneath to cook.
- Sprinkle the crumbled feta cheese over the top of the omelet.
- Fold the omelet in half with a spatula and let it cook for another minute until the cheese is melted and the eggs are fully cooked.
- Slide the omelet onto a plate and serve hot.

Grilled Tofu and Vegetable Kebabs

Grilled Tofu and Vegetable Kebabs are a healthy and delicious vegetarian option for your next barbecue or outdoor gathering. This recipe is easy to prepare, requires only a few ingredients, and can be customized to suit your taste preferences.

Ingredients:

- 1 block of firm tofu, pressed and cut into 1-inch cubes
- 1 red bell pepper, cut into 1-inch pieces
- 1 yellow squash, sliced into rounds
- 1 zucchini, sliced into rounds
- 1 red onion, cut into 1-inch pieces
- 8-10 cherry tomatoes
- 2 tbsp olive oil
- 2 tbsp balsamic vinegar
- 1 tbsp honey
- 2 garlic cloves, minced
- 1 tsp dried oregano
- 1/4 tsp salt
- Wooden or metal skewers

Instructions:

- Soak wooden skewers in water for at least 30 minutes before grilling to prevent them from burning.
- Whisk the olive oil, balsamic vinegar, honey, garlic, oregano, and salt in a small bowl.
- Thread the tofu and vegetables onto the skewers, alternating the different ingredients.
- Brush the skewers with the marinade and let them sit for at least 10 minutes to allow the flavors to meld.
- Preheat the grill to medium-high heat. Place the skewers on the grill and cook for 10-12 minutes, occasionally turning, until the vegetables are tender and lightly charred.
- Remove the skewers from the grill and serve immediately.

Carrot and Ginger Soup

Carrot and Ginger Soup is a delicious and healthy soup that is easy to make and is perfect for a light meal or as an appetizer. This soup is rich in nutrients and antioxidants, making it a great way to add vegetables to your diet.

Ingredients:

- 1 pound of carrots, peeled and chopped
- 1 small onion, chopped
- 2 cloves of garlic, minced
- 1 tablespoon of freshly grated ginger
- 4 cups of low-sodium vegetable broth
- 1 tablespoon of olive oil
- 1/4 teaspoon of black pepper
- 1/4 teaspoon of salt (optional)

Instructions:

- Heat the olive oil in a large pot over medium heat. Add the chopped onion and garlic, and sauté until they are softened.
- Add the chopped carrots and grated ginger to the pot, and stir to combine.
- Pour in the vegetable broth and bring the mixture to a boil. Reduce the heat to low and let the soup simmer for about 20-25 minutes or until the carrots are tender.
- Use an immersion blender or transfer the soup to a blender and puree until it's smooth and creamy.
- Season the soup with black pepper and salt (if using) to taste. Serve hot, and enjoy!

Cauliflower and Chickpea Salad

Cauliflower and Chickpea Salad is a healthy and delicious recipe perfect for a light lunch or as a side dish for dinner. This recipe is vegetarian, gluten-free, and low in salt and fat.

Ingredients:

- 1 head of cauliflower, cut into small florets
- 1 can of chickpeas, drained and rinsed
- 1 red bell pepper, diced
- 1 small red onion, diced
- 1/4 cup of chopped fresh parsley
- 1/4 cup of chopped fresh mint
- 1/4 cup of olive oil
- 2 tablespoons of lemon juice
- 1 teaspoon of honey
- 1/2 teaspoon of ground cumin
- 1/2 teaspoon of paprika
- Salt and pepper to taste (optional)

Instructions:

- Preheat your oven to 400°F.
- Place the cauliflower florets on a baking sheet lined with parchment paper. Drizzle with 1 tablespoon of olive oil and sprinkle with 1/4 teaspoon of salt (optional) and black pepper to taste. Roast for 20-25 minutes or until lightly browned and tender.
- Combine the roasted cauliflower, chickpeas, red bell pepper, red onion, parsley, and mint in a large bowl.
- In a small bowl, whisk together the remaining 3 tablespoons of olive oil, lemon juice, honey, cumin, paprika, and a pinch of salt (optional).
- Pour the dressing over the salad and toss gently to combine.
- Serve immediately or refrigerate until ready to serve.

DINNER RECIPES

Grilled chicken and roasted vegetables

Grilled Chicken and Roasted Vegetables are a healthy and delicious dinner option. This delicious recipe features grilled chicken and various roasted vegetables to create a nutritious, satisfying meal.
Ingredients:

- 4 breasts of boneless, skinless chicken
- 1 red bell pepper, sliced
- 1 yellow bell pepper, sliced
- 1 zucchini, sliced
- 1 yellow squash, sliced
- 1 red onion, cut
- 2 tablespoons olive oils
- 1 teaspoon garlic powder
- 1/2 teaspoon black pepper
- 1/4 teaspoon salt (optional)

Instructions:

- Pre-heat the grill to medium heat
- Combine the red onion, yellow squash, zucchini, and yellow squash in a large bowl. Toss the vegetables in olive oil, garlic powder, and black pepper.
- Place the breasts of chicken on the grill. Cook for 6-8 minutes or until internal temperature reaches 160F.
- While the chicken is heating, place the vegetables in one layer on a baking tray and bake in the oven for 15-20 minutes or until tender.
- Let the chicken cool on the grill for a while before slicing.
- Serve the grilled chicken alongside the roasted vegetables.

Steamed asparagus and broiled salmon with quinoa

This delicious and nutritious dish can help you incorporate healthier foods. The rich source of omega-3 fatty acids found in broiled salmon has been proven to improve your heart health and reduce inflammation. Quinoa, a whole grain without gluten, is rich in fiber, protein, and antioxidants. Asparagus is low in calories and high in nutrients such as folate, vitamin C, and vitamin K.

Ingredients:

- 4 salmon fillets, skin-on (4-6 oz each)
- 1 cup quinoa
- 2 cups of water
- 1 bunch of asparagus (approximately 1 lb.).
- 1 tbsp olive oil
- 1 tbsp freshly squeezed lemon juice
- 1 teaspoon garlic powder
- 1/2 teaspoon black pepper
- Salt (optional)

Instructions:

- Broiler at high heat
- Rinse the Quinoa in cold water. Drain well. Bring the water and quinoa to a boil in a large saucepan. Reduce heat to low and cover the saucepan. Let the mixture simmer for 15-20 minutes, or until the water has absorbed and the Quinoa is tender.
- Prepare the salmon while the quinoa cooks. The salmon fillets should be rinsed and dried with paper towels. After brushing each salmon fillet with olive oils, sprinkle it with garlic powder, black pepper, and a pinch of salt (if necessary).
- Place salmon fillets, skin side down, on a broiler plate. Broil the salmon for 8-10 minutes or until it is fully cooked and flaky with a fork.
- As the salmon cooks, prepare the asparagus. The asparagus should be rinsed, and the woody ends removed. The asparagus should steam for about 5-7 minutes until tender.
- Serve the cooked Quinoa by fluffing it with a fork. Divide it between four plates. Each plate should be topped with a salmon fillet, steamed asparagus spears, and a handful of steamed asparagus spears. Serve immediately with fresh lemon juice.

Grilled shrimp & vegetable kabobs

Grilled shrimp and vegetable platters are a healthy and delicious way to enjoy a light, flavorful meal. This dish is packed with nutrition and flavor. It features succulent shrimp mixed with colorful bell peppers and zucchini. For a delicious, easy-to-make meal, brush the skewers with a simple lemon juice, garlic, and olive oil marinade. Grill them to perfection until they are golden brown.

Ingredients:

- 1 lb. large shrimp, peeled, deveined
- 1 red bell pepper, seeds and cut into 1-inch pieces
- 1 yellow bell pepper, seeds and cut into 1-inch pieces
- 1 green bell pepper, seeds and cut into 1-inch pieces
- 2 medium zucchinis, cut into 1/2-inch rounds
- 1 red onion cut into 1-inch pieces
- 2 tablespoons olive oils
- 2 cloves garlic, minced
- 2 tablespoons freshly squeezed lime juice
- 1/4 teaspoon black pepper
- Salt to taste (optional).

Instructions:

- Pre-heat a grill to medium heat
- Mix the olive oil with the garlic, lemon juice, and black pepper in a small bowl. Add salt if necessary.
- Place the shrimp and vegetables on skewers. Alternate the shrimp with the vegetables.
- Make sure to coat all sides with the marinade before brushing the skewers.
- The skewers should be grilled for 2 to 3 minutes on each side or until the shrimp turn pink and opaque and the vegetables are slightly charred.
- If desired, serve the skewers warm with extra lemon wedges.

A sweet potato baked with steamed spinach, chickpeas, and chickpeas

This sweet potato baked dish is full of nutrients and flavor. It's a delicious and healthy choice for dinner. Sweet potatoes are rich in fiber, vitamin A, and potassium. Spinach and chickpeas add vitamins and protein. This recipe is low in fat and sodium, making it ideal for those who want a healthy diet.

Ingredients:

- 2 large sweet potatoes
- 1 can chickpeas, drain and rinse
- 4 cups fresh spinach
- 2 cloves minced garlic
- 2 tablespoons olive oil
- 1/4 teaspoon salt (optional).
- To taste: Black pepper

Instructions:

- Preheat the oven to 400°F (200°C).
- Clean the sweet potatoes and poke them with a fork a few times. Bake the sweet potatoes for 45-50 minutes or until tender.
- While the sweet potatoes bake, make the spinach and chickpeas. Heat 1 tablespoon olive oil in a large skillet on medium heat. Cook the minced garlic for about 30 seconds.
- Cook the chickpeas, drained and rinsed, in a skillet for 5-7 minutes, occasionally stirring until lightly browned and crisp. Set aside the chickpeas from the skillet.
- Add the olive oil and the rest of the spinach and cook in the same pan. Stirring occasionally, cook for about 2 minutes until the spinach becomes tender and wilted. Set aside the spinach from the skillet.
- After the sweet potatoes have been baked, cut them in half and season with salt and black pepper.
- Each sweet potato should be topped with chickpeas, spinach, and paprika.
- Serve and enjoy

Stir-fried chicken with vegetables and brown rice

This stir-fry recipe is delicious and healthy. This meal is excellent for meal prep or quick dinners on the weekend. It's packed with lean protein and fiber-rich vegetables.

Ingredients:

- 1 lb. boneless, skinless chicken breast cut into small cubes
- 1 tablespoon low-sodium soybean sauce
- 1 tablespoon cornstarch
- 2 tablespoons vegetable oils
- 1 red bell pepper, sliced
- 1 yellow bell pepper, sliced
- 1 small onion, cut
- 1 cup trimmed snow peas
- 1 cup grated fresh ginger
- 2 cloves garlic, minced
- 2 cups of cooked brown rice
- To taste, salt and black pepper

Instructions:

- Mix the cornstarch and soy sauce in a small bowl until well combined. Toss the chicken in the bowl. Set aside.
- Over high heat, heat a large skillet or wok. Mix 1 tablespoon vegetable oil into a large skillet or wok and swirl it to coat the bottom.
- Stir-fry the chicken in the hot oil for 2 to 3 minutes or until lightly browned. Set aside the chicken.
- The remaining tablespoon of vegetable oil should be added to the saucepan. Once the oil is hot, add the bell peppers and onion to the pan. Stir-fry the vegetables for 2 to 3 minutes or until tender.
- Stir the chicken into the pan. Continue cooking for a minute or so until the chicken is cooked through.
- Stir-fry the ingredients over brown rice. If desired, season the stir-fry with salt and pepper.

Spicy lentil soup with whole-wheat bread

This soup is hearty and delicious and makes a great healthy meal. This soup is low in sodium and fat and high in fiber, proteins, and nutrients. It makes a filling and delicious dinner when served with whole wheat bread.

Ingredients:

- 1 cup dried lentils, rinsed well and drained
- 4 cups low-sodium vegetable broth
- 1 onion chopped
- 2 cloves garlic, minced
- 1 jalapeno pepper seeded, minced
- 1 teaspoon ground cumin
- 1 tsp smoked paprika
- 1/2 tsp ground coriander
- 1/2 teaspoon ground turmeric
- 1/4 tsp cayenne pepper (optional)
- 1 can (14.5 oz) diced tomatoes, undrained
- 1 cup chopped Kale
- To taste, salt and black pepper
- 2 slices whole-wheat bread

Instructions:

- Combine the lentils, vegetable broth, and onion in a large saucepan. Add the garlic, onion, jalapeno peppers, cumin, smoked paprika, coriander, and turmeric. Bring the mixture to a boil on high heat. Reduce the heat to low and let it simmer for 20 minutes or until the lentils become tender.
- Stir in the diced tomatoes, kale, and salt in the pot. Cook the soup for another 10 minutes or until it is tender.
- Salt and black pepper are recommended to season the soup. You may not need to salt the vegetable broth.
- Toast the whole wheat bread while the soup simmers until it becomes crispy
- Serve the soup in bowls. To finish, add a slice of whole wheat toast to each bowl.

Sweet potato and baked chicken

Sweet potato and baked chicken casserole are healthy and delicious options for dinner. This meal is high in protein and fiber. The lovely sweetness of the sweet potato makes it satisfying and filling. This recipe serves 4 to 6 people.

Ingredients:

- 4 boneless, skinless chicken breasts cut into bite-sized pieces
- 2 large sweet potatoes. Peel and cut into 1-inch cubes
- 1 large onion chopped
- 2 cloves garlic, minced
- 1 teaspoon dried thyme
- 1 teaspoon paprika
- 1/4 teaspoon black pepper
- 1/4 teaspoon salt (optional)
- 1 tablespoon olive oil
- 1/2 cup low-sodium chicken broth
- 1/2 cup plain Greek yogurt
- 1/2 cup shredded cheddar cheese

Instructions:

- Preheat your oven to 375°F (190°C).
- Combine the sweet potato cubes and chicken pieces in a large bowl. Add chopped onion, minced garlic cloves, salt, pepper (if desired), and olive oil. Mix everything until sweet potatoes and chicken are well coated in oil and spices.
- In a 9x13-inch baking dish, pour the chicken broth. Spread the sweet potato and chicken mixture over the broth.
- Bake the dish with aluminum foil for 35-40 minutes or until the chicken and sweet potatoes are tender.
- Spread the Greek yogurt on top of the sweet potatoes and chicken. Sprinkle the grated cheddar cheese over the top.
- Bake the dish in the oven for another 10-15 minutes or until it is bubbly and melted.
- Allow the casserole to cool before you serve it.

Quinoa and vegetable-stuffed bell peppers

This healthy dinner recipe makes it easy to enjoy bell peppers stuffed with quinoa and other vegetables. This meal is low in fat and sodium, making it an ideal choice for those trying to live a healthy lifestyle.

Ingredients:

- 4 large bell peppers
- 1 cup quinoa
- 2 cups of water
- 1 tablespoon olive oil
- 1 small onion, chopped
- 2 cloves garlic, minced
- 1 zucchini, diced
- 1 yellow squash, diced
- 1 carrot, diced
- 1/2 teaspoon dried thyme
- 1/2 teaspoon smoked paprika
- Salt and black pepper are good for flavor

Instructions:

- Preheat the oven to 375°F (190°C).
- Remove the bell peppers' tops and the membranes. Place the bell peppers on a baking tray and let them rest.
- Bring the water and quinoa together in a saucepan. Reduce heat to medium, cover, and simmer for 15-20 minutes or until water has been absorbed and the quinoa is cooked through.
- Heat the olive oil in a large skillet on medium heat. Sauté the onion and garlic until translucent, approximately 5 minutes.
- Add the yellow squash, carrots, thyme, and smoked paprika in a skillet—season with salt and black pepper. Stir occasionally for 5 to 7 minutes or until vegetables are tender.
- Stir the cooked Quinoa into the skillet.
- Fill each bell pepper with the quinoa mixture and fill them up to the top.
- Bake the baking dish in the oven for 30 to 35 minutes or until the bell peppers and filling are tender.
- Enjoy your Quinoa and Vegetable Stuffed Bell Peppers hot!

Grilled Pork Tenderloin and Roasted Root Vegetables

This heart-healthy recipe for dinner is grilled pork tenderloin with roasted root veggies. This delicious, satisfying dish is rich in fiber and protein. It's great for any night of the week.

Ingredients:

- 1 pork tenderloin (about 1 pound)
- 2 cups mixed root vegetables (carrots, parsnips, turnips, beets, and turnips) - peeled and chopped into small pieces
- 1 small red onion, chopped and peeled
- 2 cloves garlic, minced
- 2 tablespoons olive oils
- 1/2 teaspoon dried thyme
- 1/2 teaspoon dried rosemary
- 1/2 teaspoon paprika
- Salt and black pepper are good for flavor

Instructions:

- Preheat your oven to 400°F (200°C).
- Mix the chopped root vegetables and red onions in a large bowl. Add olive oil, minced garlic, dried thyme, and rosemary to the bowl. Season with salt and pepper if necessary.
- Place the mixture in one layer on a parchment-lined baking sheet.
- Bake the vegetables for between 20-25 minutes. Stir once halfway through.
- While your vegetables are roasting, heat the grill to medium-high heat
- Season the pork tenderloin (if necessary) with salt and black pepper
- The pork tenderloin should be grilled for between 10-12 minutes. Flip halfway through.
- Allow the pork tenderloin to rest for 5-10 minutes before cutting it into rounds.
- Serve the sliced pork tenderloin with the roasted root veggies on the side.

Baked Salmon With Steamed Green Beans & Quinoa

This heart-healthy recipe provides a quick and delicious way to get your omega-3s and plenty of vegetables in one meal. For a nutritious and well-rounded dinner, bake the salmon to perfection. Serve it with steamed green beans or quinoa. It's also low in fat and sodium, making it an excellent choice for people concerned about heart health.

Ingredients:

- 4 salmon fillets, skin removed
- 1/2 teaspoon black pepper
- 1 teaspoon garlic powder
- 1/2 teaspoon onion powder
- 1/4 teaspoon salt (optional)
- 1 lb. green beans, trimmed
- 1 cup quinoa, rinsed
- 2 cups chicken broth or vegetable broth low in sodium
- 1 tablespoon olive oil

Instructions:

- Preheat the oven to 375°F (190°C).
- Season salmon fillets with onion powder, garlic powder, salt, and black pepper. Bake the salmon fillets in a baking pan for about 15-20 minutes or until they are cooked.
- While the salmon bakes, make the green beans. Bring the water to a boil in a large saucepan. Put the green beans into a steamer basket. Cover the pot with water and ensure the beans are not in direct contact with the water. Steam the beans for about 5-7 minutes or until tender but not mushy.
- Bring the broth to a boil in a large saucepan. Reduce the heat to low and add the quinoa. Allow to simmer covered for at least 15-20 minutes or until the quinoa has been cooked and the broth is absorbed.
- Use a fork to mix the quinoa and the olive oil. Mix well.
- Serve the baked salmon with steamed green beans, quinoa, and quinoa. Enjoy!

Vegetable, Lentil Curry over Brown Rice

This delicious and nutritious vegetable and lentil curry over brown rice is perfect for quick weeknight meals. This recipe is delicious and filling. It is low in fat and salt, making it a healthier choice for people watching their weight. Here's how you can make it.

Ingredients:

- 1 cup brown rice
- 2 cups of water
- 1 tablespoon olive oil
- 1 onion chopped
- 2 cloves garlic, minced
- 2 teaspoons ground cumin
- 1 teaspoon ground coriander
- 1 teaspoon ground turmeric

- 1 teaspoon ground cinnamon
- 1 teaspoon ground ginger
- 1 can (15 oz.) diced tomatoes, undrained
- 1 can (15 oz.) lentils, rinsed.
- 1 cup frozen mixed vegetables
- 1 cup chopped fresh cilantro
- Salt to your taste

Instructions:

- Rinse the brown rice, then add it to a saucepan with 2 cups water. Bring the rice to a boil. Once it has boiled, reduce the heat to low and cover the pot. Cook the rice for 35-40 minutes or until tender and all the water is absorbed.
- Heat the olive oil in a large skillet on medium heat while the rice cooks. Sauté the onion and garlic, and cook for 2 to 3 minutes until softened and translucent.
- Stir in the cumin and coriander, turmeric, and cinnamon. Continue to cook for another 1-2 minutes until the spices become fragrant.
- Stir the diced tomatoes and juice into the skillet. Let the mixture simmer for 5 minutes. Once the tomatoes are broken down, the sauce will thicken slightly.
- Stir in the frozen vegetables and lentils. Allow the curry to cook for another 5-10 minutes or until the vegetables and flavors are well combined.
- Stir in the chopped cilantro—season with salt. Enjoy the curry with brown rice.

Grilled Shrimp and Pineapple Skewers

Grilled shrimp and pineapple are delicious and healthy. They're great for picnics, outdoor parties, and weeknight meals. This low-fat and salty recipe makes it an excellent choice for people trying to reduce their sodium intake.

Ingredients:

- 1 lb. large shrimp, peeled, deveined
- 1 fresh pineapple, peeled.
- 1 red onion cut into pieces
- 1 red bell pepper, chopped into pieces
- 2 tablespoons olive oils
- 2 tablespoons honey
- 2 tablespoons of fresh lime juice
- 1 teaspoon chili powder
- 1 teaspoon garlic powder
- 1/2 teaspoon paprika
- Salt and pepper to your liking

Instructions:

- Pre-heat your grill to medium heat
- Mix the honey, olive oil, lime juice, and chili powder in a small bowl. Add the salt and pepper to taste.
- Place the shrimp, red onion, bell pepper, and pineapple on skewers.
- Make sure to brush the skewers with honey-lime marinade.
- Place the skewers on the barbecue and cook for 2 to 3 minutes or until the shrimp turn pink.
- Take the skewers off the grill and heat them.

Vegetable Stir-Fry and Baked Chicken

This recipe combines baked chicken's flavor with a vegetable stew's nutritional benefits. This is a satisfying and healthy meal you can enjoy any day of the year. You can make a delicious and balanced meal quickly with some preparation.

Ingredients:

- 4 Chicken breasts
- 1 red bell pepper, sliced
- 1 yellow bell pepper, sliced
- 1 green bell pepper, sliced
- 1 small onion, cut
- 1 tablespoon olive oil
- 1 tablespoon low-sodium soybean sauce
- 1/2 teaspoon black pepper
- 1 teaspoon garlic powder
- 1/2 teaspoon paprika
- 1/4 teaspoon salt (optional)

Instructions:

- Preheat your oven to 375°F (190°C).
- Mix the black pepper, garlic powder, and paprika in a small bowl.
- Season the chicken breasts with the spice mixture.
- Bake the chicken for 20-25 mins or until it is cooked through and no longer pink.
- While the chicken bakes, prepare the vegetables. In a large skillet, heat the olive oil on medium-high heat.
- Stir-fry the onion and peppers in the skillet for 5-7 minutes until tender but still slightly crisp.
- Stir the soy sauce into the skillet.
- After the chicken has been cooked, take it out of the oven and cut it into strips.
- Stir-fry the chicken and vegetables for 2-3 more minutes.
- If desired, serve the stir-fry with chicken and vegetables hot. Garnish it with chopped fresh herbs or lemon juice.

Sweet Potato Fries and Grilled Turkey Burgers

Sweet potato fries and grilled turkey burgers are healthy for quick lunches or dinners. This recipe is low in fat and high in flavor and nutrients. The sweet potato fries and turkey burgers are delicious and filling. This is how you make this delicious meal.

Here are the ingredients for grilled turkey burgers

- 1 lb. Ground turkey
- 1/2 cup chopped onions
- 1/4 cup chopped fresh parsley
- 1/4 cup breadcrumbs
- 1/4 cup egg whites
- 1 tablespoon Dijon mustard
- 1 teaspoon garlic powder
- 1/4 teaspoon black pepper
- Salt (optional)
- Sweet Potato Fries Ingredients:
- 2 large sweet potatoes, peeled. Cut into fries
- 1 tablespoon olive oil
- 1/2 teaspoon paprika
- 1/4 teaspoon garlic powder
- Salt (optional)
  Instructions:
- Pre-heat the grill to medium heat
- Combine the ground turkey, minced onions, chopped parsley, and breadcrumbs in a large bowl. Add egg whites, Dijon mustard garlic powder, black pepper, and a pinch of salt if necessary.
- Combine all ingredients until well combined. Form the mixture into four to six patties.
- Place the turkey patties onto the grill. Cook for about 5-6 minutes or until fully cooked.
- While the turkey burgers cook, make the sweet potato fries. Preheat the oven to 425°F. Line a baking sheet using parchment paper.
- Toss the sweet potato fries in olive oil, garlic powder, paprika, and salt in a separate bowl.
- Place the sweet potato fries in one layer on a baking sheet. Bake for 20-25 minutes or until crispy and golden brown.
- The turkey burgers can be served on a bun with your choice of toppings.

Tuna Salad with Avocado and Mixed Greens

A tuna salad with avocado, mixed greens, and various vegetables is a delicious and healthy option for light meals. This recipe combines the heart-healthy omega-3 fats found in tuna with healthy fats from avocado and nutrient-dense greens. This salad will boost your energy levels and provide your daily doses of vitamins and minerals.

Ingredients:

- 2 cans tuna, drained
- 1 avocado, diced
- 2 cups mixed greens
- 1/4 cup diced red onions
- 1/4 cup chopped fresh cilantro
- 1 tablespoon freshly squeezed lime juice
- 1 tablespoon extra-virgin olive oils
- Salt and pepper to your liking
- Optional: Sliced cucumber, sliced red onion, cherry tomatoes, or any other vegetable you like for extra nutrition and flavor.

Instructions:

- Start by prepping the ingredients. Set aside the tuna. Chop the red onion, avocado, and cilantro.
- Mix the chopped cilantro, red onion, and greens in a large bowl. Mix well.
- Mix the tuna with the water in a bowl. Add it to the bowl and mix well.
- Mix the olive oil, lime juice, salt, and pepper in a small bowl.
- Toss the tuna salad ingredients in the dressing and drizzle the sauce.
- Add the diced avocado to the tuna salad mix and gently stir to combine.
- Serve the tuna salad right away, with optional cilantro and sliced cucumber.

Broiled Cod with Roasted Brussels Sprouts

Broiled cod with roasted Brussels Sprouts is an excellent choice for a healthy and delicious weeknight meal. This recipe is low on fat and salt, which makes it a perfect choice for those who want to eat healthier but not sacrifice flavor.

Ingredients:

- 4 cod fillets (about 6 oz each)
- 1 lb. Brussels sprouts, cut and halved
- 1 tbsp olive oil
- 1 teaspoon garlic powder
- 1/2 tsp smoked paprika
- 1/2 teaspoon dried oregano
- 1/4 teaspoon black pepper
- 1/4 tsp salt (optional)
- For serving, lemon wedges

Instructions:

- Preheat your oven to 400°F
- Toss the Brussels sprouts in olive oil, garlic powder, and smoked paprika on a baking sheet. Add salt if necessary. Place them evenly on a baking sheet.
- The Brussels sprouts can be roasted in the oven for 25-30 minutes or until tender and golden brown.
- While the Brussels sprouts roast, make the cod. Season the fillets with a pinch of black pepper and some salt if necessary.
- Turn the broiler on high. Place the cod fillets, skin-side down, on a broiler plate.
- Bake the cod for 8-10 mins or until it is fully cooked and has a light brown crust.
- Serve the broiled cod alongside the roasted Brussels sprouts, lemon wedges, and a side dish of mashed potatoes.

Baked Turkey Meatballs and Zucchini Noodles

This recipe offers a healthier alternative to traditional spaghetti and meatballs. You can substitute zucchini noodles for pasta and use baked turkey meatballs for a lower-calorie option. These meatballs can be a tasty and nutritious addition to any meal.

Ingredients for the meatballs

- Ground turkey 1 lb. lean
- 1/2 cup breadcrumbs
- 1/4 cup grated Parmesan cheese
- 1/4 cup finely chopped onions
- 1 egg
- 2 cloves garlic, minced
- 1 teaspoon dried oregano
- 1/2 teaspoon dried basil

- 1/2 teaspoon black pepper
- 1/4 teaspoon salt (optional)
  To make zucchini noodles:
- 4 medium zucchinis
- 2 tablespoons olive oil
- 2 cloves garlic, minced
- 1/4 teaspoon red pepper flakes (optional).
- Salt and black pepper are good for flavor

Instructions:

- Preheat the oven to 350F
- Combine the ground turkey, Parmesan cheese, and breadcrumbs in a large bowl. Add the onion, egg yolk, garlic, oregano basil, black pepper, salt, and salt (if applicable). Combine all ingredients with your hands until well combined.
- Make small meatballs from the mixture (about 1 tablespoon each) and place them on parchment paper-lined baking sheets.
- Bake the meatballs in the oven for 18-20 minutes or until they are well browned.
- While the meatballs bake, make the zucchini noodles. To create thin noodles-like strips of zucchini, use a spiralizer.
- In a large nonstick skillet, heat the olive oil on medium heat. Sauté the garlic and red pepper flakes, if any, for about 1-2 minutes until fragrant.
- Toss the zucchini noodles in the skillet with the oil and garlic mixture. Cook the noodles for 2 to 3 minutes or until tender but still slightly crispy.
- Season the zucchini noodles with salt, black pepper, and to your liking.
- If desired, serve the baked turkey meatballs with zucchini noodles. Garnish with Parmesan cheese or fresh herbs.

Grilled Chicken & Vegetable Kebabs

The healthy and delicious grilled chicken and vegetable kebabs can be prepared in any season. These kebabs are easy to prepare and customizable. They can be eaten separately or accompanied by rice or salad. We will be using boneless chicken breasts in this recipe. Various colorful vegetables will also be used to enhance the flavor and nutrition of the kebabs. We will use minimal salt and fat to keep this recipe healthy.

Ingredients:

- 1 lb. boneless, skinless chicken breast. Cut into bite-size pieces
- 1 red bell pepper, chopped into bite-sized pieces
- 1 yellow bell pepper, chopped into bite-sized pieces
- 1 zucchini, cut into rounds
- 1 red onion, chopped into bite-sized pieces
- 8-10 wooden skewers, soaked for 30 minutes in water
- 1/4 cup olive oil
- 2 tablespoons lemon juice
- 2 cloves of garlic, minced
- 1 teaspoon dried oregano
- 1/2 teaspoon black pepper
- 1/4 teaspoon salt (optional)

Instructions:

- Preheat grill to medium-high heat
- Mix olive oil, lemon zest, minced garlic, and dried oregano in a small bowl. Add salt if necessary.
- You will thread the vegetables and chicken onto the skewers. To ensure even cooking, leave a little space between each piece.
- Make sure to brush the kebabs with the marinade.
- Place the kebabs on a preheated grill. Cook for 12-15 minutes, turning once or twice, or until the chicken and vegetables are fully cooked.
- Serve the kebabs hot from the grill with your favorite side dish.

Curry with Shrimp and Vegetables over Brown Rice

This a delicious, healthy, and quick recipe for shrimp and vegetable stir-fry with brown rice. This delightful dish is high in protein, fiber, and vitamins and can be served as a lunch or dinner.

Ingredients:

- 1 lb. Shrimp, deveined and peeled
- 2 tbsp. Olive oil
- 1 red bell pepper, sliced
- 1 green bell pepper, sliced
- 1 yellow onion, cut
- 2 cups broccoli florets
- 2 cloves of garlic, minced
- 2 tsp. Ginger, grated
- 1/4 cup low-sodium soy sauce
- 1 tbsp. Honey
- 1 tbsp. 1 tbsp. cornstarch
- 2 tbsp. 2 tbsp.
- 4 cups of cooked brown rice

Instructions:

- Place a large skillet on medium heat—1 tbsp. Add 1 tbsp—olive oil to your skillet.
- Cook the shrimp in the skillet until they turn pink. Set aside the shrimp.
- Add another tablespoon of oil to the same skillet. Add the bell peppers and onion to the skillet. Let the vegetables cook for about 3-4 minutes or until tender-crisp.
- Cook the ginger and garlic in a skillet for another 1-2 mins.
- Mix the honey, cornstarch, and soy sauce in a small bowl. Add a pinch of salt if necessary.
- Return the shrimp to the skillet. Pour the soy sauce over the shrimp and vegetables and stir to combine.
- Continue cooking for another 1-2 mins until the sauce thickens.
- Serve the shrimp and vegetable stir-fry over a bed of brown rice.

Baked Eggplant With Tomato and Mozzarella Cheese

Baked eggplant with tomato and mozzarella cheese is a healthy and delicious dish for light lunches or dinners. Easy to prepare, this dish is full of flavor and nutrients. Eggplants are low-calorie and high in fiber. Tomatoes are rich in vitamin C and lycopene. Mozzarella cheese gives the word a creamier touch.

Ingredients:

- 1 large eggplant
- 2 medium-sized tomatoes
- 1/2 cup shredded mozzarella cheese
- 1 tablespoon olive oil
- 1 teaspoon garlic powder
- 1/2 teaspoon dried basil
- 1/2 teaspoon dried oregano
- 1/4 teaspoon black pepper
- Salt to taste (optional).

Instructions:

- Preheat the oven to 350F
- Cut the eggplant into rounds of 1/2 inch thickness. Sprinkle each slice with salt, if desired. Place them on parchment paper-lined baking sheets. Bake the eggplant for 15 minutes or until it is slightly browned.
- Slice the tomatoes into thin rounds while the eggplant bakes.
- Mix the olive oil, garlic powder, and basil in a small bowl. Add the black pepper, salt, oregano, and oregano if necessary.
- After the eggplant has been baked, take it out of the oven and let it cool down.
- Broil the oven.
- Place the slices of eggplant in one layer on a baking sheet. Add a few pieces of tomato to each slice.
- Apply the olive oil mixture to each tomato and slice of eggplant.
- Sprinkle mozzarella cheese on top of each slice.
- Broil the baking sheet under the broiler for 2 to 3 minutes or until the cheese has melted.
- Take the baking sheet out of the oven and allow it to cool down before serving.

Slow-Cooker Vegetable Soup

Slow-cooker chicken soup with vegetable soup is hearty and nutritious. It's great for cold days or when you feel under the weather. This recipe is low-fat and high in lean protein.

Ingredients:

- 1 lb. boneless, skinless chicken breasts cut into bite-sized pieces
- 4 cups low-sodium chicken broth
- 1 onion chopped
- 2 cloves of garlic, minced
- 2 carrots, peeled & chopped
- 2 celery stalks chopped
- 1 cup frozen corn
- 1 cup frozen peas
- 1 teaspoon dried thyme
- 1 bay leaf
- Salt and black pepper are good for flavor

Instructions:

- Combine the chicken, broth, and onion in a 6-quart slow cooker. Add celery, carrots, sticks, onions, garlic, and peas. Mix well.
- Cook the chicken on low for 6-8 hrs. or high for 3-4 hours until tender.
- Take the bay leaf out of the slow cooker and throw it away.
- Use a slotted spoon to remove approximately 1 cup of the chicken and vegetables from the slow cooker—place in a blender/food processor. Blend until smooth.
- Mix in a slow cooker. Stir to combine.
- Season the soup with black pepper and salt to taste. Use a little salt to start, then add more as needed.
- If desired, serve hot with fresh herbs and shredded cheese.

Grilled Steak With Roasted Peppers & Onions

Grilled steak served with onions, roasted peppers, and onions is an excellent choice for any occasion. This recipe is quick and easy and only requires a few ingredients. It's a perfect option for quick and healthy meals.

Ingredients:

- 1 lb. sirloin steak
- 1 large red onion, cut
- 2 red bell peppers, sliced
- 2 tbsp olive oil
- 2 tbsp balsamic vinegar
- 1 teaspoon garlic powder
- 1/2 teaspoon black pepper
- 1/4 tsp salt (optional)

Instructions:

- Pre-heat the grill to medium heat
- Season the steak with black pepper and garlic powder.
- Use 1 tablespoon of olive oil to brush the steak.
- Grill the steak for about 4-5 minutes or until you are satisfied with the doneness.
- Let the steak rest on the grill for 5-10 minutes before slicing it.
- Place the steak in a pan and heat it on medium heat.
- The remaining olive oil should be added to the skillet. Next, add the chopped onions and peppers.
- Stirring occasionally, cook the peppers and onions for 8-10 minutes until softened and slightly charred.
- Mix the balsamic vinegar and the skillet. Stir to combine.
- Continue to cook the peppers and onions for 2-3 minutes or until the vinegar is absorbed.
- Top the steak with roasted peppers, onions, and sliced steak.

Baked Chicken with Vegetable Casserole

A healthy and delicious recipe for a family dinner, baked chicken and vegetable casserole makes a great choice. The dish is loaded with fresh vegetables and flavorful chicken. It also has a mix of herbs and spices to make your taste buds scream for more. It's also low in fat and salt, making it an excellent choice for people trying to reduce their sodium intake and calories.

Ingredients:

- 4 boneless, skinless chicken breasts cut into bite-sized pieces
- 2 cups chopped mixed vegetables (e.g., carrots, broccoli, and cauliflower)
- 1 medium onion chopped
- 2 cloves garlic, minced
- 1 teaspoon dried thyme
- 1 teaspoon dried oregano
- 1/2 teaspoon paprika
- 1/4 teaspoon black pepper
- 1/4 teaspoon salt (optional)
- 1/4 cup low-sodium chicken broth
- 1/4 cup plain Greek yogurt
- 1/4 cup grated Parmesan cheese

Instructions:

- Preheat your oven to 375°F (190°C).
- Heat 1 tablespoon olive oil in a large skillet on medium heat. Cook the chicken pieces until golden brown, approximately 5-7 minutes. Transfer the chicken to a 9x13-inch baking dish.
- Add another tablespoon of olive oil to the skillet and cook the onion for 5 minutes. Sauté the minced garlic for 30 seconds more
- Place the chopped vegetables in a skillet. Cook for approximately 5-7 minutes until they become slightly tender.
- Stir in the black pepper, dried thyme, and paprika in the skillet.
- Bring the chicken broth to a boil in a saucepan. Once it has boiled, reduce heat to medium-low.
- Turn off the heat in the skillet and add the Greek yogurt and grated Parmesan cheese.
- Spread the vegetable mixture evenly over the chicken.
- Bake the casserole for 20-25 mins, or until the vegetables and chicken are tender.
- If desired, serve the casserole hot with fresh herbs garnished.

Lentil, Vegetable Stir-Fry Over Brown rice

Lentil and vegetable stir fry over brown rice are delicious and nutritious. It is also easy to make and can be enjoyed by vegetarians and vegans. This dish contains fiber, protein, nutrients, and vitamins from vegetables and lentils. It is also a healthy option for dinner.

Ingredients:

- 1 cup brown rice
- 1 can lentil (15 oz).
- 2 tbsp olive oil
- 2 cloves garlic, minced
- 1 onion, diced
- 1 bell pepper, diced
- 2 carrots, sliced
- 2 cups broccoli florets
- 1 cup mushrooms, sliced
- 1 tbsp low-sodium soy sauce
- 1 tablespoon lemon juice
- 1 teaspoon paprika
- 1/2 teaspoon black pepper
- Salt to taste (optional).

Instructions:

- Brown rice should be cooked according to package instructions.
- Drain the lentils and rinse them under running water.
- Heat the olive oil on medium heat in a large saucepan.
- Sauté the minced garlic, onion, and onion until translucent.
- Add the diced bell peppers, chopped carrots, broccoli, and sliced mushrooms to the pan. Stir fry the vegetables for about 5-7 minutes or until tender but still slightly crisp.
- Stir-fry the lentils in the pan for 3-4 minutes.
- Mix the low-sodium soybean sauce, lemon juice, and paprika in a small bowl. Add salt if necessary.
- Stir-fry ingredients together with the sauce.
- Serve the vegetable and lentil stir-fry with brown rice.

Grilled Shrimp and Mixed Vegetables

Grilled shrimp with mixed vegetables is a healthy and delicious dish for any occasion. This dish is low in fat and salt, making it an excellent choice for people trying to reduce their intake of nutrients. This recipe features fresh shrimp grilled to perfection, paired with various nutritious and colorful vegetables.

Ingredients:

- 1 lb. large shrimp, deveined and peeled
- 1 red bell pepper, sliced
- 1 yellow bell pepper, sliced
- 1 zucchini, sliced
- 1 yellow squash, sliced
- 1 red onion, cut
- 2 tablespoons olive oil
- 2 tablespoons lemon juice
- 2 cloves minced garlic
- 1/4 teaspoon black pepper
- 1/4 teaspoon salt (optional).
- 8 wooden skewers

Instructions:

- Before grilling, soak the wooden skewers for 30 minutes in water.
- Pre-heat the grill to medium heat
- Mix the olive oil with lemon juice, minced garlic, and black pepper in a small bowl. Add salt if necessary.
- Place the vegetables and shrimp on the skewers.
- Use the olive oil mixture to brush the skewers.
- Place the skewers on the barbecue and cook for 2 to 3 minutes per side or until the shrimp and vegetables are cooked through.
- Serve immediately after removing the skewers.

Baked Salmon and Roasted Asparagus with Quinoa

A healthy and delicious recipe for any occasion is baked salmon with roasted asparagus and quinoa. With a simple seasoning, the salmon is baked to perfection. The quinoa and roasted asparagus provide a healthy and delicious side dish. This easy recipe will impress your guests.

Ingredients:

- 4 fillets of salmon
- 1 bunch asparagus
- 1 cup quinoa
- 2 cups water
- 1 lemon
- 2 tablespoons olive oil
- 1 teaspoon garlic powder
- 1 teaspoon paprika
- Salt and pepper to your liking

Instructions:

- Preheat the oven to 400°F (200°C).
- Put the quinoa through a fine mesh strainer. Add it to a medium saucepan with two cups of water. Bring to a boil. Then reduce heat to low and cover the saucepan. Let the mixture simmer for 15-20 minutes or until all the water is absorbed and the Quinoa is tender. Set aside.
- Rinse the asparagus, and then cut off any woody ends. Place the asparagus on a parchment-lined baking sheet. Sprinkle with 1 tablespoon of olive oil. Season with salt and pepper as needed. Bake in the oven for 12-15 mins or until tender.
- As the asparagus roasts, prepare the salmon. The salmon fillets should be rinsed and dried with paper towels. Mix 1 tablespoon olive oil, garlic powder, and paprika with salt and pepper in a small bowl. The mixture should be rubbed over salmon fillets.
- After the asparagus has been cooked, take it out of the oven and place it in a bowl. Turn the stove to 450°F (230°C).
- Place the salmon fillets, skin-side down, on the same baking sheet with the asparagus. Bake the salmon in the oven for 12-15 minutes or until it is flaky with a fork.
- Drizzle the lemon juice on the asparagus as the salmon bakes and toss it to coat.
- Serve the baked salmon with quinoa and roasted asparagus. Enjoy!

Grilled Chicken With Vegetable And Quinoa Salad

Grilled Chicken With Vegetable And Quinoa Salad can be prepared in minutes and is healthy and nutritious. It is excellent for lunch and dinner. This recipe makes a delicious and satisfying meal that doesn't require any extra salt or fat. Grilled chicken is served with a colorful and delightful quinoa salad topped with fresh vegetables.

Ingredients:

- Grilled Chicken
- 2 breasts of boneless, skinless chicken
- 1 tsp. 1 tsp. garlic powder
- 1 tsp. smoked paprika
- 1 tsp. 1 tsp. dried oregano
- 1/2 tsp. 1/2 tsp.
- 1 tbsp. Olive oil
  For the Quinoa and Vegetable Salad:
- 1 cup quinoa, rinsed
- 2 cups of water

- 1/2 diced red onion
- 1 red bell pepper, chopped
- 1 yellow bell pepper, chopped
- 1 zucchini, diced
- 1 cup chopped fresh parsley
- 1 cup chopped fresh mint
- 1/4 cup fresh lemon juice
- 1 tbsp. Olive oil
- Salt and pepper to your liking

Instructions:

- Preheat grill to medium-high heat
- Mix the garlic powder, olive oil, dried oregano, and smoked paprika in a small bowl. The spice mixture should be applied to the chicken breasts.
- Grill the chicken on both sides for 6-8 minutes or until it is fully cooked.
- Combine the quinoa with water in a medium saucepan. Bring to a boil. Then reduce heat to low, cover, and cook for 15-20 minutes. Cook for 15-20 minutes or until water is absorbed and the quinoa is tender.
- Combine the cooked quinoa with red onion, red, yellow, and green bell peppers, zucchini, and parsley in a large bowl. Season it with salt, pepper, lemon juice, olive oils, and salt. Combine all ingredients.
- Grill the chicken with the vegetable and quinoa salad.

Baked Tofu With Sauteed Kale And Mushrooms

This healthy and delicious vegan recipe for baked tofu with sauteed kale and mushrooms is great for quick dinners. This recipe is high in protein and nutrients. It's low in fat and salt, making it a good choice for people trying to eat healthier.

Ingredients:

- Baked Tofu
- 1 block firm tofu, drain, and press
- 1 tablespoon low-sodium soybean sauce
- 1 tablespoon maple syrup
- 1 tablespoon olive oil
- 1 teaspoon smoked paprika
- 1 teaspoon garlic powder

- Sauteed Kale & Mushrooms
- 1 bunch of kale. Stems removed. Chop.
- 1 cup sliced mushrooms
- 1/2 cup chopped onion
- 2 cloves minced garlic
- 1 tablespoon olive oil
- Salt and pepper to your liking

Instructions:

- Preheat the oven to 350F. Place parchment paper on a baking sheet.
- Make small cubes of tofu and place them in an eclair.
- Mix the soy sauce and maple syrup in a separate bowl. Add the olive oil, olive oil, smoked paprika, garlic powder, and olive oil.
- Toss the sauce on top of the tofu cubes.
- Place the tofu cubes on the baking sheet.
- Bake the tofu in the oven for 20-25 minutes or until it is crispy and golden brown.
- While the tofu bakes, prepare the sauteed mushrooms and kale while the tofu's still warm.
- Place the olive oil in an oven-proof skillet on medium heat.
- Sauté the onion and garlic until fragrant, approximately 2-3 minutes
- Continue to saute the mushrooms until tender, around 5-7 minutes.
- Sauté the chopped kale in a skillet until it becomes tender and wilted, approximately 3-5 minutes.
- Salt and pepper to your liking

Broiled Scallops with Roasted Root Vegetables

A healthy and delicious recipe for seafood that can be grilled with roasted root veggies is broiled scallops. This mouthwatering combination of sweet and savory root veggies and tender, juicy scallops creates a delicious dish full of flavor and low in fat.

Ingredients:

- 1 lb. Fresh scallops
- 1 lb. Mixed root vegetables (carrots, parsnips, turnips, beets, etc.)
- 2 tbsp. Olive oil
- 1 tsp. 1 tsp. dried thyme
- 1/2 tsp. garlic powder
- 1/2 tsp. paprika
- 1/4 tsp. black pepper
- Optional: 1/4 tsp. Salt

Instructions:

- Preheat your oven to 400°F (200°C).
- Cut your root vegetables into small pieces. Spread the vegetables in one layer on a baking tray. Drizzle olive oil, garlic powder, paprika, and salt (if necessary). Mix the spices and toss the vegetables.
- Bake the vegetables for between 25-30 minutes. Stir occasionally until tender and lightly browned.
- While the vegetable roast, make the scallops. Then rinse them under cold water. Dry them with a towel. If necessary, remove the small muscle at the end of each scallop.
- Season the scallops with black pepper and paprika pinch, then place them on a parchment-lined baking sheet or broiler pan.
- The scallops should be boiled on each side for 2 to 3 minutes or until golden brown on both sides.
- Place the roasted root veggies on a plate, then top them with the broiled scallops. If desired, garnish with lemon wedges or fresh herbs.

Grilled Chicken with Vegetable and Chickpea Stew

Grilled chicken and vegetables with chickpea and chickpea soup is a delicious and healthy meal. It combines tender chicken with hearty vegetables and chickpeas stew. This meal is rich in protein, fiber, and essential nutrients and makes a good choice for a balanced meal. The recipe is simple to prepare, and everyone will enjoy it.

Ingredients:

- 4 breasts of boneless, skinless chicken
- 1 can chickpeas, drain, and rinse.
- 1 diced red onion
- 2 bell peppers (red or yellow, or orange), diced
- 2 medium zucchinis, diced
- 4 cloves garlic, minced
- 1 can dice tomatoes

- 1 tsp. smoked paprika
- 1/2 tsp. Cumin
- 1/2 tsp. 1/2 tsp.
- 1/4 tsp. 1/4 tsp.
- 1/4 tsp. salt (optional)
- 2 tbsp. Olive oil
- For garnish, fresh parsley or cilantro can be chopped.

Instructions:

- Pre-heat your grill to medium heat
- Season the chicken breasts with cumin, black pepper, oregano, and some salt (optional). Use a little olive oil to brush the breasts of the chicken.
- Grill the breasts of chicken for 6-8 minutes on each side or until they reach 165°F.
- While the chicken is heating, make the vegetable and chickpea soup. Heat 2 tbsp olive oil in a large saucepan or Dutch oven. Heat 2 tbsp olive oil on medium heat
- Sauté the minced garlic and diced red onions for 2 to 3 minutes, until softened.
- Sauté the zucchini and diced bell peppers in the pot for another 5-10 minutes until they soften.
- Add diced tomatoes, rinsed chickpeas, smoked paprika, and cumin to the potto the pot. Mix well.
- Let the stew simmer for 10-15 minutes, occasionally stirring until the vegetables become tender.
- After the chicken has been cooked, take it off the grill and let it cool for a while before cutting it into pieces.
- Divide the chickpea and vegetable stew among four bowls and top each bowl with grilled chicken. If desired, garnish with chopped cilantro or parsley.

ONLY VEGETARIAN MAIN COURSE RECIPES

Lentil soup with vegetables and Quinoa

This lentil soup recipe is hearty, nutritious, and delicious. It is excellent for cold days. It's heart-healthy because it includes quinoa and other vegetables.

Ingredients:

- 1 cup dried green lentils. Rinsed and drained.
- 1/2 cup quinoa, rinsed
- 1 tablespoon olive oil
- 1 medium onion chopped
- 2 cloves of garlic, minced
- 2 celery stalks, chopped
- 2 carrots, diced
- 1 teaspoon ground cumin
- 1/2 teaspoon smoked paprika
- 1/4 teaspoon black pepper
- 6 cups low-sodium vegetable broth
- 1 cup chopped Kale
- 1 tablespoon of lemon juice

Instructions:

- Heat the olive oil in a large saucepan or Dutch oven on medium heat. Cook the olive oil over medium heat until the carrots, onion, celery, garlic, and celery are tender, approximately 5 minutes.
- Stir in the cumin, smoked pepper, and black pepper until the vegetables are well coated.
- Add the lentils and quinoa to the vegetable broth. Bring to a boil. Reduce heat to low, and simmer for 20-25 mins until lentils and Quinoa are tender.
- Add the chopped kale and lemon juice and stir. Continue to cook for 5 minutes more until the kale has wilted.
- Adjust the seasoning by tasting and adding salt (up to 1/2 teaspoon). If desired, serve hot, garnished with chopped kale and fresh herbs.

Spicy Vegetable Chili

This chili is rich in nutritious vegetables and protein-rich black beans. It has a spicy kick to warm you up when it's cold outside. This chili recipe is low in fat and salt. It's an excellent option for anyone who wants to enjoy comforting chili without worrying about their health.

Ingredients:

- 1 tablespoon olive oil
- 1 large onion chopped
- 3 cloves garlic, minced
- 1 chopped red bell pepper
- 1 green bell pepper chopped
- 1 jalapeno pepper seeded, finely chopped
- 2 teaspoons ground cumin
- 2 teaspoons chili powder
- 1 teaspoon smoked paprika
- 1/2 teaspoon black pepper
- 2 cans (every 15 ounces) of black beans, drain, and rinse.
- 1 can (28 ounces) crushed tomatoes
- 1 cup vegetable broth
- 1 tablespoon tomato paste
- 1 cup corn kernels
- 2 tablespoons chopped fresh cilantro
- Salt to taste (optional).

Instructions:

- Heat the olive oil in a large saucepan on medium heat. Sauté the onion and garlic until softened and translucent. This takes about five minutes.
- Continue to saute the green and red bell peppers and the jalapeno pepper for 5 more minutes or until the peppers become tender.
- Mix the cumin and chili powder with the smoked paprika and black pepper in a pot. Stir well to combine.
- Mix the tomato paste, black beans, crushed tomatoes, and vegetable broth into the pot. Stir to combine.
- The chili should be brought to a boil. Once the chili is simmering, reduce the heat to low and cover the pot. Let the chili simmer for 30 minutes, stirring now and again.
- Stir the corn into the pot. Let the chili simmer for 10 more minutes until it is hot.
- Mix in the chopped cilantro and season with salt if necessary.
- If desired, serve the chili hot with extra cilantro or shredded cheese.

Stuffed Eggplant in Greek Style with Feta Cheese

Easy to prepare, Greek-style stuffed eggplants with feta cheese are a tasty and healthy vegetarian main dish. This recipe is full of flavor and nutrients, making it an excellent choice for a satisfying and healthy meal.

Ingredients:

- 4 medium eggplants
- 1 onion chopped
- 2 cloves garlic, minced
- 1 chopped red bell pepper
- 1/2 cup quinoa
- 1/2 cup water
- 1 tablespoon olive oil
- 1 tablespoon dried oregano
- 1/2 teaspoon ground black pepper
- 1/2 cup crumbled Feta cheese
- 2 tablespoons chopped fresh Parsley

Instructions:

- Preheat the oven to 375°F (190°C).
- Slice the eggplants in half along the lengthwise. Then scoop out the flesh and leave a 1/2-inch shell. The eggplant flesh can be chopped and left to rest.
- Heat the olive oil in a large skillet on medium heat. Sauté the onion, garlic, and red bell pepper until softened and fragrant.
- Add the chopped eggplant flesh, quinoa, and water to a skillet. Mix well.
- Bring the mixture to a boil. Then reduce heat to low and cover the skillet. Let the mixture simmer for 15-20 minutes or until the quinoa has become tender and the liquid is absorbed.
- Mix in the crumbled Feta cheese and chopped Parsley.
- Place the quinoa mixture in the eggplant shells, and then bake them.
- Bake the casserole in foil for 30-40 minutes or until tender.
- Bake for another 5-10 minutes to brown the cheese top.
- Take the stuffed eggplants out of the oven. Let them cool down for a while before you serve.

Chickpea, Vegetable Stir-Fry

This stir-fry for vegetarians is a delicious and healthy way to get your daily intake of vegetables and protein. Chickpeas (garbanzo beans) are an excellent plant-based protein and fiber source. This recipe is perfect for weeknight dinners because it's quick and straightforward.

Ingredients:

- 1 can chickpeas (15oz), rinsed and drained
- 1 red bell pepper, sliced
- 1 yellow bell pepper, sliced
- 1 large carrot, peeled & sliced
- 1 small onion, cut
- 1 tablespoon olive oil
- 2 cloves garlic, minced
- 1 teaspoon ground cumin
- 1/2 teaspoon smoked paprika
- 1/4 teaspoon black pepper
- 1/4 teaspoon salt (optional)
- Fresh parsley chopped (for garnish).

Instructions:

- Olive oil over medium heat in a large skillet
- Sauté the garlic and onion sliced until translucent, approximately 2-3 minutes.
- Sauté the carrot and pepper slices in a skillet until tender, about 5-7 minutes.
- Mix chickpeas with ground cumin, smoked paprika, black pepper, and salt in a skillet. Stir to combine.
- To heat the vegetables and chickpeas, saute for 2-3 more minutes.
- Serve warm, garnished with fresh parsley.

Vegan Shepherd's Pie With Lentils And Sweet Potatoes

Vegan Shepherd's Pie With Lentils and Sweet Potatoes is a healthy and hearty dish that's great for anyone who follows a plant-based diet. This dish contains protein, fiber, complex carbohydrates, and other vital nutrients for maintaining a healthy heart. This dish is low in sodium and fat, making it an excellent choice for people trying to reduce their salt intake.

Ingredients:

- 3 medium sweet potatoes, peeled. Cut into small cubes
- 1 tablespoon olive oil
- 1 onion chopped
- 2 cloves of garlic, minced
- 1 carrot, chopped and peeled
- 2 celery stalks chopped
- 1 chopped red bell pepper
- 1 cup green lentils or brown lentils, rinsed well and drained
- 2 cups vegetable broth
- 1 teaspoon dried thyme
- 1 teaspoon paprika
- 1 teaspoon ground cumin
- Salt and pepper to your liking
- 2 tablespoons chopped fresh Parsley (optional).

Instructions:

- Preheat the oven to 375°F (190°C).
- Cook the sweet potatoes in a large saucepan of boiling water for 15 minutes or until tender. Drain the sweet potatoes and place them in a bowl.
- Heat the olive oil in a large skillet on medium heat. Sauté the onion and garlic until translucent.
- Sauté the bell pepper, carrot, and celery in a skillet for 5 minutes or until they are softened slightly.
- Add the lentils, vegetable broth, thyme, paprikas, cumin, salt, and pepper in a large skillet. Bring the mixture to a boil. Reduce the heat and simmer the mixture for approximately 20-25 minutes, or until the lentils have been cooked and the mixture thickens.
- Mix the sweet potatoes in a large bowl until smooth.
- Place the lentil mixture in a 9-inch (23cm) baking dish. Add the mashed sweet potato mixture to the lentil mixture.
- Bake the Shepherd's Pie in the oven for 25-30 minutes or until the sweet potatoes turn golden brown.
- Before serving, sprinkle chopped parsley on top.

Spinach and Mushroom Lasagna

A delicious main dish that's healthy and filling is mushroom and spinach lasagna. This lasagna recipe includes layers of noodles, sauteed spinach, and a creamy low-fat cheese sauce. This dish is excellent for preparing for weeknight meals or special occasions.

Ingredients:

- 12 lasagna noodles (whole grain, if possible).
- 8 oz mushrooms, sliced
- 4 cups fresh spinach, chopped
- 2 tbsp olive oil
- 2 tbsp all-purpose flour
- 2 cups of low-fat milk
- 1/4 teaspoon garlic powder
- 1/4 teaspoon black pepper
- 1/4 teaspoon salt
- 1/4 tsp nutmeg
- 8 oz low-fat ricotta cheese
- 1/4 cup grated Parmesan cheese
- 1/4 cup chopped fresh parsley

Instructions:

- Preheat the oven to 375°F (190°C). Follow the package directions to cook lasagna noodles until they are al dente. Drain and then set aside.
- Sauté the sliced mushrooms in 1 tablespoon olive oil in a large skillet on medium heat until tender and golden brown. Set the mushrooms aside from the skillet.
- Add another tablespoon of olive oil to the skillet and cook the chopped spinach until it is wilted. Set aside the spinach.
- Mix the flour, 1/2 cup of milk, and the salt in a small saucepan until smooth. Slowly whisk in the rest of the milk, garlic powder, black pepper, salt, and nuts. Mix the mixture on medium heat and continuously whisk until it thickens.
- Combine the grated Parmesan, ricotta, and chopped parsley in a bowl.
- Spread 1/2 cup cheese sauce on the bottom of a 9x13-inch baking dish. Spread 4 lasagna noodles on top of the sauce. Spread half the ricotta cheese mixture on the noodles. Layer half the sauteed mushrooms, spinach, and remaining ricotta over the noodles. Sprinkle 1 cup of cheese sauce on top of the vegetables. Continue the layers with the rest of the noodles, the ricotta cheese mixture, mushrooms, and the cheese sauce.
- Bake the lasagna in the oven for 25 minutes by covering it with foil. Bake the lasagna for an additional 15-20 minutes.
- Let the lasagna cool for 10-15 minutes before cutting and serving.

Ratatouille With Quinoa

Ratatouille with Quinoa, a heart-healthy vegetarian main course, is excellent for light lunches or dinners. This classic French dish has tomatoes, eggplants, zucchini, onions, and peppers. We will use quinoa to add texture and protein to this recipe. This recipe is low on salt and fat, making it an excellent choice for healthy meals.

Ingredients:

- 1 large eggplant, cut into cubes
- 2 medium zucchinis, cut into cubes
- 1 red bell pepper, sliced
- 1 chopped yellow onion
- 2 cloves of garlic, minced
- 1 can diced tomatoes (14oz)
- 1 cup quinoa
- 2 cups water
- 1 tablespoon olive oil
- 1 teaspoon dried thyme
- 1 teaspoon dried rosemary
- Salt and pepper to your liking

Instructions:

- Preheat the oven to 375°F (190°C).
- Heat the olive oil in a large skillet on medium heat. Sauté the garlic and onion until softened for about 3-4 minutes.
- Continue to cook the bell pepper, zucchini, and eggplant for approximately 5 minutes, stirring occasionally.
- Add the can of diced tomatoes, rosemary, and thyme to the skillet. Mix well.
- Salt and pepper to your liking. Don't add too much salt to canned tomatoes that may already have it.
- Bake the mixture in a baking dish for 25-30 minutes until the vegetables are tender.
- While the ratatouille bakes, prepare the quinoa. Then, rinse the quinoa with a fine mesh strainer. Bring to a boil. Reduce heat to low and cover the saucepan. Let it simmer for 15-20 minutes or until the quinoa becomes tender and the water has been absorbed.
- Enjoy the ratatouille with the cooked Quinoa.

Vegetarian Bibimbap With Brown Rice and Vegetables

Vegetarian Bibimbap is a Korean delight that's both delicious and healthy. It is packed with colorful vegetables and brown rice making it a nutritious meal. This dish is low in fat and salt, making it an excellent choice for those with heart problems.

Ingredients:

- 2 cups cooked brown rice
- 4 eggs
- 1 cup shredded carrots
- 1 cup sliced cucumbers
- 1 cup sliced mushrooms
- 2 cups spinach
- 4 tablespoons low-sodium soybean sauce
- 4 tablespoons sesame oil
- 4 teaspoons gochujang sauce (Korean red chili paste)
- 1 tablespoon vegetable oil

Instructions:

- Brown rice should be cooked according to package directions.
- Heat the vegetable oil in a saucepan on medium heat. Sauté the mushrooms in the vegetable oil for 3-4 minutes or until lightly browned.
- Sauté the spinach in the pan for 2-3 minutes until it is wilted.
- Fry the eggs in a separate skillet until they are cooked to your liking.
- Divide the brown rice among four bowls
- Add equal quantities of sauteed mushrooms, spinach, shredded carrots, and sliced cucumbers to each rice bowl.
- Each bowl should be coated with 1 teaspoon of low-sodium soybean sauce, 1 teaspoon of sesame oil, and 1 teaspoon of gochujang sauce.
- Add a fried egg to each bowl.
- Serve and enjoy

Zucchini and Eggplant Gratin

A delicious vegetarian dish, eggplant and zucchini gratin are excellent for heart-healthy meals. This dish is low in fat and salt, making it a perfect choice for people trying to reduce their fat and salt intake. This is an easy way to add more vegetables to your diet.

Ingredients:

- 1 large eggplant, cut into 1/4-inch rounds
- 2 medium zucchinis, sliced into 1/4-inch rounds
- 1 onion chopped
- 2 cloves garlic, minced
- 2 tablespoons olive oils
- 1/2 teaspoon dried thyme
- 1/2 teaspoon dried basil
- 1/2 teaspoon dried oregano
- 1/4 teaspoon black pepper
- 1/4 cup grated Parmesan cheese
- 1/4 cup breadcrumbs
- 2 tablespoons chopped fresh Parsley

Instructions:

- Preheat the oven to 350 degrees Fahrenheit
- Heat the olive oil in a large skillet on medium heat. Sauté the garlic and chopped onion for 2 to 3 minutes or until translucent.
- Place the zucchini and eggplant slices in a skillet. Cook for about 5-7 minutes or until slightly softened.
- Stir in the black pepper, dried thyme, and basil in the skillet.
- Spread the vegetable mixture in a 9x13 inch baking pan and evenly distribute it.
- Combine the breadcrumbs and grated Parmesan cheese in a small bowl.
- Sprinkle the Parmesan cheese and breadcrumb mix over the vegetables.
- Bake the gratin for 30 to 35 minutes in the oven or until the top turns golden brown and the vegetables become tender.
- Place the gratin in the oven. Sprinkle the chopped parsley on top.
- Let the gratin cool down for a while before you serve it.

Vegetable Curry and Vegan Lentil

Vegetable curry and Vegan Lentil are hearty main dishes rich in plant-based protein, fiber, and vitamins. This recipe is excellent for meal prep or weeknight meals. It can be made in large batches and kept in the refrigerator for several days.

Ingredients:

- 1 cup green lentils or brown lentils, rinsed well and drained
- 1 tbsp olive oil
- 1 medium onion, diced
- 3 minced garlic cloves
- 1 tbsp grated fresh Ginger
- Ground cumin: 2 tsp
- 1 tsp ground coriander
- 1 teaspoon turmeric
- 1/2 teaspoon cinnamon
- 1/2 teaspoon cayenne pepper (optional; adjust to your taste).
- 1 can (14 oz.) diced tomatoes with juice
- 2 cups low-sodium vegetable broth
- 1 small cauliflower cut into florets
- 2 medium carrots, sliced
- 1 small zucchini, sliced
- 1 small red bell pepper, chopped
- 2 cups baby spinach, washed and chopped
- 1 cup chopped fresh cilantro
- Salt and pepper to taste

Instructions:

- Heat the olive oil in a large saucepan or Dutch oven on medium heat. Cook the onion, garlic, and ginger for 5 minutes.
- Stir in the turmeric, cumin, coriander, and cinnamon. Continue cooking for another 1-2 minutes.
- Add the diced tomatoes, their juice, vegetable broth, and lentils. Bring to a boil. Reduce heat to low, and simmer covered for 20-25 minutes or until lentils become tender.
- Add the red bell pepper, cauliflower, carrots, and zucchini to the pot. Simmer the vegetables for 10-15 minutes or until tender but not mushy.
- Stir in the chopped spinach and cilantro, and cook until the spinach is tender. Season the dish with salt and pepper according to your taste.
- If desired, serve the curry hot with brown rice or whole-wheat naan bread.

Spinach and Mushroom Stuffed Portobello Mushrooms

Stuffed portobello mushrooms make a delicious and hearty vegetarian main dish. This healthy, satisfying meal features savory mushrooms, creamy ricotta, and flavorful spinach. They are quick and easy to prepare, making them a great weeknight meal.

Ingredients:

- 4 large portobello mushrooms, stems & gills removed
- 2 cups fresh spinach, chopped
- 1/2 cup ricotta cheese
- 1/4 cup grated Parmesan cheese
- 1/4 cup chopped onion
- 2 cloves garlic, minced
- 1 tablespoon olive oil
- 1/4 teaspoon salt (optional)
- 1/4 teaspoon black pepper

Instructions:

- Preheat oven to 375°F (190°C).
- Heat olive oil in a large skillet on medium heat. Sauté onion and garlic until softened and fragrant, approximately 2-3 minutes.
- Cook the spinach in a skillet until it is wilted. Turn off the heat.
- Combine the cooked spinach with ricotta cheese and parmesan cheese in a bowl. Season with salt and pepper if necessary. Combine all ingredients.
- Place the portobello mushroom on a parchment- or silicone-lined baking sheet.
- Fill each mushroom cap with the spinach mixture and fill them up to the top.
- Bake the stuffed mushroom in the oven for 20-25 mins or until tender.
- Take the cake out of the oven and allow it to cool down before serving.

Quinoa and Vegetable Roast

A delicious, healthy main course for vegetarians that can be eaten at lunch or dinner is the roasted vegetable and quinoa salad with Feta cheese. This recipe is high in nutrients, fiber, and protein and low in fat. It is easy to make, and you can add your favorite vegetables.

Ingredients:

- 1 cup quinoa
- 2 cups of water
- 1 small eggplant, chopped and cut into small pieces
- 1 red bell pepper chopped into small pieces
- 1 zucchini chopped into small pieces
- 1/2 Red onion chopped into small pieces
- 2 tablespoons olive oils
- 1/2 teaspoon salt
- 1/4 teaspoon black pepper
- 1/2 cup crumbled Feta cheese
- 2 tablespoons chopped fresh parsley

Instructions:

- Preheat the oven to 400°F (200°C).
- Rinse the Quinoa in a fine mesh strainer. Bring the water to a boil on medium heat.
- Reduce heat to low and cover the saucepan with a lid. Let the saucepan simmer for 15-20 minutes or until water has been absorbed and the Quinoa is tender. Set aside.
- Combine the red bell pepper, zucchini, and eggplant in a large bowl. Toss the vegetables in olive oil, salt, and black pepper.
- Place the vegetables in one layer on a parchment-lined baking sheet. Bake in the oven for 25-30 minutes or until the vegetables are tender.
- Combine the cooked quinoa with the roasted vegetables in a large bowl. Toss in the crumbled feta cheese and chopped parsley, and gently mix.
- Warm or at room temperature, serve the quinoa and roasted vegetable salad.

Vegetable Stir-Fry with Brown Rice

A nutritious, heart-healthy, easy-to-make meal is tofu and vegetable stir fry with brown rice. It is excellent for busy weeknights. This recipe is low in fat, sodium, protein, and fiber.

Ingredients:

- 1 block firm tofu, drained then cubed
- 1 red bell pepper, sliced
- 1 yellow bell pepper, sliced
- 1 zucchini, sliced
- 1 small onion, cut
- 2 cloves minced garlic
- 1 tablespoon olive oil
- 2 tablespoons low-sodium soybean sauce
- 1 tablespoon cornstarch
- 1/4 cup water
- 1/4 teaspoon black pepper
- 2 cups cooked brown rice

Instructions:

- Place the olive oil in an oven-proof skillet on medium heat.
- Cook the tofu in a skillet until it is golden brown. Stir occasionally. Set the tofu aside from the skillet.
- Add bell peppers, zucchini, and onion in a skillet, and cook for 5-7 minutes or until tender-crisp.
- Cook the minced garlic in a skillet for 1-2 minutes or until fragrant.
- Mix the low-sodium soybean sauce, cornstarch, and water in a small bowl. Add the black pepper.
- Place the tofu in a skillet. Add the soy sauce to the skillet.
- Stir fry for 2-3 minutes or until the sauce thickens.
- Serve the vegetable and tofu stir-fry with the brown rice.

Vegan Sweet Potato and Bean Enchiladas

Vegan Sweet Potato and Black Bean Enchiladas make a delicious and healthy meal. Soft tortillas are filled with sweet potatoes, black beans, and spices. Then, the dish is topped with an enchilada sauce that makes it bubbly.

Ingredients:

Filling:

- 2 large sweet potatoes, peeled & diced
- 1 can of black beans, drained. Rinsed.
- 1 chopped red onion
- 1 chopped red bell pepper
- 1 tsp smoked paprika
- 1 teaspoon ground cumin
- 1/2 tsp chili powder
- 1/4 teaspoon black pepper
- 1/4 tsp salt (optional)
- 2 tbsp olive oil

The enchilada sauce:

- 2 tbsp olive oil
- 2 Tbsp flour
- 2 tbsp chili powder
- 1 teaspoon ground cumin
- 1/4 teaspoon garlic powder
- 1/4 teaspoon onion powder
- 2 cups vegetable broth
- Salt (optional)

For assembly:

- 8-10 soft tortillas
- Shredded vegan cheese (optional).
- Cilantro chopped
- Lime wedges

Instructions:

- Preheat the oven to 375°F (190°C).
- Heat the olive oil in a large skillet on medium heat. Then add the sweet potatoes and red onion. Cook the vegetables for about 10 minutes.
- Add the black beans, smoked paprika, and chili powder to the pot. Season with salt, if necessary. Cook an additional 5 minutes, stirring now and again.
- While the filling cooks, make the enchilada salsa. Heat the olive oil in a small saucepan on medium heat. Mix the oil with the flour until it is smooth. Mix in the chili powder and ground cumin. Add the garlic powder and onion powder and mix well. Slowly add the vegetable broth. Whisk constantly to avoid lumps. Let the sauce cook for about 5-10 minutes until it thickens. Salt to taste, if necessary.
- Place the enchilada Sauce on the bottom of a 9x13-inch baking pan.
- Assemble the enchiladas by spooning the filling onto each tortilla. Place the tortilla seam-side down on the baking tray. Continue this process until all tortillas have been filled and rolled.
- Spread the remaining enchilada Sauce over the top of the rolled-up Tortillas. Sprinkle vegan cheese if desired.
- Bake the baking dish covered with foil for 20-25 minutes until it is hot and bubbly.
- Let cool in the oven for a few minutes before removing from the oven. Serve with lime wedges and garnish with cilantro.

Grilled Vegetables and Feta Cheese Skewers

This delicious vegetarian dish is great for summer barbecues and weeknight meals. These skewers are made from various colorful vegetables marinated in a simple, flavorful dressing. They are then grilled to perfection and topped with crumbled Feta cheese. This heart-healthy dish is low in fat and salt but full of nutrients.

Ingredients:

- 2 zucchinis, cut into rounds
- 2 yellow squashes, cut into rounds
- 1 red onion cut into pieces
- 1 red bell pepper, chopped into pieces
- 1 yellow bell pepper, chopped into pieces
- 1/4 cup olive oil
- 2 tablespoons balsamic Vinegar
- 1 teaspoon dried oregano
- 1 teaspoon garlic powder
- 1/4 teaspoon black pepper
- 1/2 teaspoon salt (optional)
- 1/2 cup crumbled Feta cheese

Instructions:

- Pre-heat your grill to medium heat
- Mix the olive oil with balsamic vinegar, garlic powder, black pepper, and oregano in a small bowl.
- Place the vegetables on skewers and alternate between them.
- Make sure to coat the skewers with the dressing.
- Place the skewers on the barbecue and cook for 5-7 minutes or until the vegetables are tender.
- Take the skewers off the grill and add the crumbled Feta cheese to the top.
- Serve the skewers as soon as they are hot.

Spinach, Ricotta Stuffed Shells With Marinara Sauce

Spinach and Ricotta, Stuffed Shells with Marinara Sauce, is a healthy and delicious vegetarian main dish for a hearty meal. This dish is made with jumbo pasta shells stuffed with spinach, ricotta, and other flavorful ingredients. Then, they are baked in a marinara sauce. This easy recipe is low in fat and salt, making it an excellent choice for heart health. It will also impress your guests.

Ingredients:

- 24 jumbo pasta shells
- 1/2 cup part-skim ricotta
- 1 cup chopped spinach
- 1/2 cup grated Parmesan cheese
- 1 egg
- 1 tablespoon olive oil
- 1 clove minced garlic
- 1/4 teaspoon black pepper
- 1/4 teaspoon salt (optional).
- 2 cups marinara sauce

Instructions:

- Preheat your oven to 350°F
- Follow the instructions on the package to cook the pasta shells. Drain the pasta and rinse it with cold water until cool.
- Combine the ricotta cheese with chopped spinach, grated Parmesan, egg, olive oils, minced garlic, black, and salt in a large bowl. Combine all ingredients until well combined.
- Place a thin layer of marinara sauce in the bottom of a 9x13-inch baking dish.
- Each pasta shell should be filled with the spinach and ricotta mixture. Place the stuffed shells one by one in the baking dish.
- Place the remaining marinara sauce on top of the stuffed shells.
- Bake the dish with aluminum foil for 25-30 minutes or until the shells are cooked and the sauce bubbles.
- Continue baking for 5-10 minutes or until cheese is melted.
- Take the cake out of the oven and allow it to cool down before serving.

Bean Chili with Quinoa and Vegetable

Vegetables and bean chili made with quinoa are delicious and healthy. This dish is high in protein, fiber, essential vitamins, minerals, and other nutrients, making it a satisfying and healthy meal.

Ingredients:

- 1 cup quinoa. Rinse and drain.
- 2 cups vegetable broth
- 1 tablespoon olive oil
- 1 large onion chopped
- 2 bell peppers chopped
- 2 medium carrots, chopped
- 4 cloves garlic, minced
- 1 tablespoon chili powder
- 1 teaspoon ground cumin
- 1 teaspoon paprika
- 1/4 teaspoon cayenne pepper
- 1 can (14.5 ounces) diced tomatoes, undrained
- 1 can (15 ounces) of kidney beans, rinsed.
- 1 can (15 ounces) of black beans, rinsed.
- 1 can (15 ounces) corn, drained
- 1 cup chopped fresh cilantro
- Salt and pepper to taste

Instructions:

- Combine the quinoa with the vegetable broth in a large saucepan. Bring to a boil. Then reduce heat to low, cover, and simmer for 15-20 minutes. Allow to simmer for 15-20 minutes or until the quinoa has become tender and the broth is absorbed.
- Heat the olive oil in a large saucepan or Dutch oven on medium heat. Cook the bell peppers, onions, and carrots for about 5-7 minutes or until tender.
- The garlic, cumin powder, cumin, and cayenne pepper should be added to the pot. Let it simmer for about 1-2 minutes or until fragrant.
- Add the kidney beans, black beans, and diced tomatoes to the pot. Mix well.
- The mixture should come to a boil. Once the mixture has boiled, reduce the heat to low. Cover the variety and cook for 20-30 minutes or until the vegetables and flavors are well combined.
- Mix in the cooked Quinoa and chopped cilantro—salt and pepper to taste.
- Serve warm, garnished with extra cilantro if desired.

Mushrooms and Lentil Shepherd's Pie

The mushroom and lentil shepherd's pies are a delicious, nutritious vegetarian option to traditional meat-based dishes. This hearty, satisfying meal is rich in fiber, protein, flavor, and nutrition. This recipe is low in fat and salt, making it healthier.

Ingredients:

Filling:

- 2 tablespoons olive oils
- 1 large onion, diced
- 2 cloves garlic, minced
- 8 oz mushrooms, sliced
- 1 cup of cooked lentils
- 1 cup frozen peas
- 1 tablespoon tomato paste
- 1 tablespoon all-purpose flour

- 1 teaspoon dried thyme
- 1/2 teaspoon black pepper
- 1/4 teaspoon salt (optional)

Topping:
- 2 pounds russet potatoes, peeled & chopped
- 1/4 cup unsweetened almond buttermilk
- 2 tablespoons vegan butter
- 1/4 teaspoon black pepper
- 1/4 teaspoon salt (optional)

Instructions:

- Preheat your oven to 375°F (190°C).
- Heat the olive oil in a large skillet on medium heat. Sauté the chopped onion and minced garlic for 3-4 minutes until translucent.
- Place the sliced mushrooms in a skillet. Cook for about 5-7 minutes until they are tender and release their juices.
- Add the cooked lentils, frozen peas, all-purpose flour (if necessary), dried thyme, black olives, and salt. Stirring occasionally, cook for 2 to 3 minutes until the mixture is well-combined and the flour is evenly distributed.
- Transfer the mushroom-lentil mixture to a 9-inch (23 cm) baking dish.
- Boil the potatoes in a large saucepan until tender (about 15 minutes).
- Drain the potatoes and then return them to their original pot. Add the unsweetened almond milk, vegan butter, black pepper, salt, and salt (if applicable). Mix the potatoes until smooth and creamy
- Spread the mashed potatoes on top of the mushroom and lentil mixture. Smoothen the surface with a spatula.
- Bake the shepherd's pie for 20-25 minutes until the top is lightly golden brown and the filling bubbles.
- Allow the pie to cool before you serve it.

Vegan Stuffed Peppers with Quinoa and Black Beans

Easy-to-make vegan stuffed peppers with black beans and quinoa are delicious and nutritious. This recipe is excellent for a low-fat, low-salt dish that still packs much flavor. Although the recipe is easy, it is imposing and will be loved by vegans and non-vegans. Here's how it is made:

Ingredients:

- 4 large bell peppers
- 1 cup quinoa. Rinse and drain.
- 1 can of black beans, drained. Rinsed.
- 1 onion, diced
- 2 cloves of garlic, minced
- 1 tablespoon olive oil
- 1 teaspoon ground cumin
- 1/2 teaspoon smoked paprika
- Chili powder 1/4 teaspoon
- 1/4 teaspoon black pepper
- 1 cup chopped fresh cilantro
- One lime juice

Instructions:

- Preheat the oven to 350°F (190°C). Place parchment paper on a baking sheet.
- Remove the tops from the bell peppers. Place the peppers on the baking sheet.
- Bring 2 cups of water to a boil in a large saucepan. Reduce the heat to medium and add the quinoa. Cook for 15-20 minutes until the water has been absorbed and the rice is tender. Set aside.
- Heat the olive oil in a large skillet on medium heat. Sauté the onion and garlic for 5-7 minutes or until softened and translucent.
- Mix in the black beans, cumin, and smoked paprika. Add 1/4 teaspoon salt (optional). Stir and continue cooking for another 5 to 7 minutes.
- Stir the cooked Quinoa into the skillet. Continue to cook for 2-3 minutes or until all is well heated.
- Stir in the lime juice and chopped cilantro.
- Fill the bell peppers with the quinoa-black bean mixture. Bake the stuffed peppers on a baking sheet for 25-30 minutes or until they are softened and lightly browned.
- Let the stuffed peppers cool in the oven for a few minutes before removing them from the oven.

Hummus Wrap and Roasted Vegetable

A delicious, healthy, and tasty roast vegetable and hummus wrap can be enjoyed at any hour of the day. This combination of roasted vegetables, homemade Hummus, and a tortilla wrap creates a delicious, nutritious meal rich in nutrients.

Ingredients:

- 1 medium zucchini cut into bite-sized pieces
- 1 medium red bell pepper chopped into bite-sized pieces
- 1 medium-sized yellow bell pepper, cut into bite-sized pieces
- 1 small red onion chopped into bite-sized pieces
- 1 tbsp olive oil
- 1/2 teaspoon salt
- 1/4 teaspoon black pepper

- 1/2 cup homemade Hummus (see the recipe below).
- 4 Whole Wheat Tortilla Wraps
Homemade Hummus
- 1 can (15 oz.) chickpeas, drain and rinse
- 2 cloves garlic, minced
- 1/4 cup tahini
- 1/4 cup lemon juice
- 2 tbsp olive oil
- 1/4 teaspoon salt
- 1/4 teaspoon cumin

Instructions:

- Preheat the oven to 400°F
- Mix the chopped zucchini, red bell pepper, yellow bell pepper, and red onions in a large bowl. Add the olive oil, salt, and black pepper to coat.
- Place the vegetables in one layer on a baking tray and roast for 20-25 minutes. Stir occasionally until tender.
- Make the homemade hummus while the vegetable roast. Combine the chickpeas with garlic, lemon juice, olive oils, salt, and cumin in a food processor. Blend until smooth. Scrape down the sides as necessary.
- After the roasted vegetables, take them out of the oven and allow them to cool.
- Spread 2 tablespoons of homemade hummus on each tortilla wrap to assemble it.
- Place the roasted vegetables in equal portions on the wraps and place them on the hummus.
- Wrap the wraps tightly and tuck in the ends.
- Serve immediately

Vegetable Stew and Vegan Lentil

Vegan Lentil and Vegetable Stew are delicious and hearty dishes perfect for a relaxing night. This stew contains protein, fiber, essential vitamins, and minerals. You can customize this stew by adding your favorite veggies and spices.

Ingredients:

- 1 cup dried green or brown lentils
- 2 cups water
- 1 tablespoon olive oil
- 1 onion chopped
- 3 cloves minced garlic
- 2 chopped carrots
- 2 stalks of celery, chopped
- 1 sweet potato, peeled.
- 1 can diced tomatoes (14oz)
- 4 cups vegetable broth
- 1 teaspoon paprika
- 1 teaspoon cumin
- 1/2 teaspoon salt (optional).
- 1/4 teaspoon black pepper
- 2 cups chopped spinach or kale
- Fresh parsley to garnish

Instructions:

- Rinse the lentils under a strainer. Place them aside.
- Heat the olive oil on medium heat in a large saucepan or Dutch oven.
- Sauté the onion for 3-4 minutes until translucent.
- Add the sweet potato, carrots, and celery to the pan. Continue to saute for 5-6 minutes until the sweet potato is slightly softened.
- Mix the diced tomatoes with the water and stir.
- Add the pot's lentils, water, vegetable broth, and salt.
- Mix in the cumin, salt, and black pepper.
- Bring the stew to a boil. Then reduce heat to low and cover the pot.
- Let the vegetables and lentils simmer for 25-30 minutes, until tender.
- Mix in the chopped spinach or kale and cook for another 5-10 minutes, until tender.
- Season as necessary.
- Serve warm, garnished with fresh parsley.

Chickpea Curry and Cauliflower

A delicious, healthy, tasty vegetarian dish made with cauliflower and chickpeas is cauliflower and chickpea curry. This curry is excellent for entertaining a large group or as a weeknight meal. This dish is filling and satisfying thanks to the combination of tender cauliflower florets with protein-packed chickpeas. The curry sauce is made using a variety of coconut milk and warm spices. It has a creamy, slightly sweet taste. This recipe is low in fat and salt, making it an excellent choice for people trying to reduce their sodium intake and calories.

Ingredients:

- 1 head of cauliflower cut into small florets
- 1 can chickpeas, drain and rinse
- 1 onion, diced
- 3 cloves minced garlic
- 1 tablespoon grated fresh ginger
- 1 teaspoon ground cumin
- 1 teaspoon ground coriander
- 1 teaspoon turmeric
- 1/2 teaspoon paprika
- 1/4 teaspoon cayenne pepper (optional) for spicier curry
- 1 can of coconut milk
- 1 tablespoon olive oil
- Salt to taste (optional).

Instructions:

- Heat the olive oil in a large skillet or Dutch oven on medium heat. Cook the diced onion until translucent for about five minutes.
- Cook the minced garlic, grated ginger, and water for 2 minutes. Stir occasionally.
- Stir the onion mixture into the cauliflower florets and add them to the skillet. Cook the cauliflower for about 5-7 minutes until it is softened.
- If necessary, stir the spices (cumin, coriander, turmeric, and paprika) into the skillet.
- Stir the coconut milk into the skillet. Let the mixture simmer for 10-15 minutes until the cauliflower is tender.
- Stir the chickpeas into the skillet. Allow the mixture to cook for 5-10 minutes or until the chickpeas become tender.
- If you like the curry, taste it and adjust the salt to suit your tastes.
- Hot cauliflower and chickpea curry

Spinach, Feta, and Feta Cheese Stuffed Mushrooms

Spinach and Feta cheese stuffed mushrooms make a healthy side dish or appetizer everyone can enjoy. This recipe combines the rich flavor of mushrooms with creamy feta cheese and the fresh taste of spinach. This dish is excellent for people looking to eat healthier but still enjoy delicious flavors.

Ingredients:

- 12 mushrooms of medium size
- 2 cups fresh spinach, chopped
- 1/2 cup crumbled Feta cheese
- 1/4 cup grated Parmesan cheese
- 2 cloves garlic, minced
- 1/4 teaspoon black pepper
- 1/4 teaspoon salt
- 1 tbsp olive oil

Instructions:

- Preheat the oven to 350F
- Remove the mushroom stems and wipe the caps clean with a damp cloth. Place the mushrooms cap-side down in a baking dish.
- Mix the chopped spinach, Parmesan cheese, grated Parmesan cheese, and minced garlic in a medium bowl. Add salt.
- Place the spinach and feta cheese mixture in each mushroom cap. Press down to fill it.
- Olive oil can be used to drizzle the stuffed mushrooms.
- Bake the stuffed mushroom mixture for 20-25 minutes or until the cheese is melted.
- If desired, serve the spinach and feta cheese-stuffed mushrooms warm, garnished with Parmesan cheese or chopped parsley.

Vegetarian Mushroom and Spinach Quiche

This delicious vegetarian mushroom and spinach quiche recipe can be a healthy choice for anyone looking to cut back on meat or enjoy a nutritious, savory meal. This quiche is delicious and filling and can be made with fresh ingredients such as spinach, eggs, and mushrooms. It can also be used for dinner.

Ingredients:

- 1 pie crust pre-made (store-bought, homemade).
- 6 large eggs
- 1 cup milk (or milk alternative)
- 1/2 teaspoon salt
- 1/4 teaspoon black pepper
- 2 cups baby spinach, washed and chopped
- 1 cup chopped mushrooms
- 1/2 cup shredded cheddar cheese
- 1 tablespoon olive oil
- 1 clove minced garlic

Instructions:

- Preheat the oven to 375°F (190°C).
- Pre-made pie crust, roll out, and place in a 9-inch pie plate.
- Mix the eggs, milk, and salt in a large bowl. Set aside.
- In a large skillet, heat the olive oil on medium heat. Sauté the minced garlic for 1 minute until fragrant.
- Place the mushrooms in a skillet. Cook for 5-7 minutes until tender and slightly browned.
- Cook the chopped spinach in a skillet for 2-3 minutes until it is wilted.
- Spread the mushroom-spinach mixture onto the pie crust and spread it evenly.
- Spread the egg mixture on top of the vegetables.
- Sprinkle the cheddar cheese on top of the quiche.
- Bake the quiche for 35-40 mins, or until the top is golden brown.
- Let cool in the oven for about 10-15 minutes before slicing. Enjoy your delicious vegetarian spinach and mushroom quiche!

Vegan Roasted Vegetable & Chickpea Pasta Salad

This is a healthy and delicious way to enjoy a satisfying meal full of vegetables and plant protein. The vegetables are roasted to bring out their natural sweetness, and the chickpeas give the pasta a creamy texture. This recipe is low in fat and salt, making it an excellent choice for those who want to eat healthier.

Ingredients:

- 1 pound pasta (preferably whole-grain)
- 1 chopped red bell pepper
- 1 chopped yellow bell pepper
- 1 zucchini, chopped
- 1 eggplant chopped
- 1 can chickpeas, drain and rinse
- 1/4 cup olive oil
- 2 cloves minced garlic
- 1 tablespoon dried oregano
- 1/2 teaspoon black pepper
- 1/2 teaspoon salt (optional).

Instructions:

- Preheat the oven to 400°F (200°C). Place parchment paper on a baking sheet.
- Combine the chopped vegetables, chickpeas, and olive oil in a large bowl. Add salt (if necessary). Mix everything and toss.
- Spread the chickpea and vegetable mixture on a baking sheet in one layer.
- The vegetables can be roasted in the o 25-30 minutes or until tender. To ensure even toasting, stir the vegetables at least once.
- While the vegetable roast, prepare the pasta according to the package instructions. Rinse the pasta under cold water.
- After the roasted vegetables and chickpeas, add them to the pasta and toss them to combine.
- If desired, serve hot with fresh herbs and grated Parmesan cheese.
- Enjoy your healthy and delicious roasted vegetable or chickpea pasta

DESSERT

Berry and Yogurt Parfait

This Berry and Yogurt Parfait is a healthy and delicious dessert that will satisfy your sweet tooth without ruining your diet. This parfait is rich in protein, fiber, and antioxidants. It's made with fresh berries and low-fat yogurt. It's simple to prepare and customize with your favorite toppings and fruits.

Ingredients:

- 1 cup plain low-fat yogurt
- 1/2 cup fresh berries (such as strawberries, blueberries, or raspberries)
- 1/4 cup granola
- 1 teaspoon honey (optional).

Instructions:

- Rinse the fresh berries and cut them into bite-sized pieces.
- Place a layer of yogurt in the bottom of a glass or parfait dish.
- Sprinkle some chopped berries over the yogurt.
- Spread granola on top of the berries.
- Continue to add layers until you reach the top.
- If desired, drizzle honey over the top of the granola
- Serve immediately, or let cool in the fridge until you are ready to eat.

Baked Apples With Cinnamon

Baked Apples With Cinnamon are a tasty and simple dessert. This dessert is low in fat and salt and only uses natural ingredients. It's warm and comforting and packed with fiber and antioxidants.

Ingredients:

- 4 medium-sized apples
- 1 Tablespoon cinnamon
- 1 tablespoon honey
- 1/2 teaspoon salt (optional).

Instructions:

- Preheat your oven to 375°F (190°C).
- Core and wash the apples. Either use an apple corer or a knife to remove the body. Leave 1/4 inch of the apple at the bottom to hold the filling.
- Mix the honey, cinnamon, and salt in a small bowl.
- Use a spoon to stuff the cavities of the apples with the cinnamon-honey mix.
- Bake the apples in a baking tray for about 30-40 minutes or until they are tender and the filling bubbles.
- Warm the baked apples with vanilla yogurt or chopped nuts if you like.

Banana Oat Cookies

Banana Oat Cookies make a delicious and healthy dessert. They are low in sugar, high in fiber, and low in fat. This recipe is vegan and gluten-free. It's suitable for all dietary requirements. These cookies can be made quickly and enjoyed as a snack or dessert.

Ingredients:

- 2 ripe bananas, mashed
- 1 1/2 cups rolled oatmeal
- 1/2 teaspoon cinnamon
- 1/4 teaspoon salt
- 1/4 cup chopped nuts (optional).
- 1/4 cup raisins (optional)
- Optional 1/4 cup dark chocolate chips

Instructions:

- Preheat the oven to 350°F (180°C). Line a baking sheet using parchment paper.
- Mix the bananas in a large bowl until smooth.
- Mix the cinnamon, rolled oatmeal, salt, and salt in a bowl. Stir until combined.
- Mix chopped nuts, raisins, or dark chocolate chips until well combined.
- Drop the dough onto the baking sheet with a cookie scoop or spoon. Flatten each cookie with the back of a spoon.
- Bake the cookies for 12-15 minutes or until they are lightly golden on the edges and fully set.
- Let cool in the oven for a while, then transfer to a wire rack. These healthy and delicious cookies are great for snacking or dessert.

Dark Chocolate Covered Strawberries

Dark Chocolate Covered Strawberries are a classic dessert that's both delicious and healthy. This sweet and healthy recipe will satisfy your sweet tooth but not compromise your health. Dark chocolate contains antioxidants that can reduce inflammation and improve heart health. Fresh strawberries are high in fiber, vitamin A, and other good nutrients for your heart.

Ingredients:

- 1 pint of fresh strawberries, washed and dried
- 1/2 cup dark chocolate chips or chopped dark chocolate
- 1/4 tsp sea salt (optional)

Instructions:

- Place a sheet of parchment paper on a large plate or baking sheet.
- Mix the dark chocolate in a double boiler or microwave. Stir every 30 seconds until it is completely melted.
- Salt can be added to the chocolate after melting.
- Take a strawberry and hold it by the stem. Dip it in the melted chocolate and swirl it around to coat it evenly.
- Remove the strawberry from the chocolate, and let any excess chocolate drip back into your bowl.
- Place the strawberry covered in chocolate on the parchment paper.
- Continue with the rest of the strawberries until they are covered in chocolate.
- The baking sheet or plate should be kept in the fridge for 10-15 minutes or until the chocolate is set.
- After the chocolate has set, the strawberries can be served immediately or kept in the refrigerator for up two days.

Chia Seed Pudding

Chia seed pudding is a healthy and delicious dessert that can be made in minutes and customized with many toppings. This recipe is vegan and gluten-free.

Ingredients:

- 1/4 cup chia seeds
- 1 cup unsweetened almond buttermilk
- 1/2 tsp vanilla extract
- 1/2 teaspoon cinnamon
- Salt pinch (optional).

Instructions:

- Combine chia seeds with almond milk, vanilla extract, and cinnamon in a bowl. Add salt if necessary.
- Mix all ingredients until combined.
- Cover the bowl with plastic wrap and let it cool in the refrigerator for at least two hours or overnight. Stir occasionally.
- Give it a final stir once the pudding has thickened and the chia seed has absorbed all the liquid.
- Serve the pudding in a bowl or jar and garnish with your favorite fruits, nuts, seeds, or nuts.

Grilled Pineapple

Grilled Pineapple makes a delicious and simple dessert, perfect for summer gatherings. This delightful, sweet, and tangy dish can be used as a substitute for traditional sugary desserts. It requires only a few ingredients. This heart-healthy recipe is for grilled pineapple with minimal salt and fat.

Ingredients:

- 1 fresh pineapple
- 1 tablespoon honey
- 1 cup fresh lime juice
- 1 teaspoon ground cinnamon
- Salt pinch (optional).

Instructions:

- Pre-heat your grill to medium heat
- Cut off the top and bottom ends of the pineapple. Then, remove the skin and core.
- Slice the pineapple into slices of 1/2 inch thickness
- Mix the honey, lime juice, and cinnamon in a small bowl. Add a pinch of salt if necessary.
- Use the honey mixture to brush both sides of each slice of pineapple.
- Place the pineapple slices on the grill. Cook for 3-4 minutes or until grill marks appear on each side.
- Take the pineapple slices off the grill and warm them.

Lemon Sorbet

Lemon sorbet makes a refreshing, light dessert perfect for hot summer days. This recipe is simple to prepare and does not contain any added fat. It is an excellent option for people trying to reduce their fat intake.

Ingredients:

- 1 cup of fresh lemon juice (about 6 lemons).
- 1 cup water
- 1/2 cup honey
- Salt pinch (optional).

Instructions:

- Combine the honey and water in a small saucepan. Heat on medium heat. Stir until honey dissolves.
- Turn off the heat and allow it to cool to room temperature.
- Mix the honey syrup and lemon juice in a large bowl.
- Place the mixture in a small dish and freeze.
- After one hour, take the dish out of the freezer. Use a fork or a spoon to scrape the mixture.
- For the next 2 to 3 hours, repeat the process for 30 minutes. Continue this process until the sorbet has fully frozen and is slushy.
- Serve immediately, or transfer to a container that is airtight and place in the freezer.

Mixed Berry Crisp

Mixed Berry Crisp is a nutritious and delicious dessert that showcases the best summer berries. This recipe uses fresh berries, almond flour, oats, and honey. This recipe is easy to prepare and a healthy alternative to classic fruit crisp.

Ingredients:

Filling:

- 3 cups of mixed fresh berries (such as blueberries, raspberries, and blackberries).
- 1 tablespoon honey
- 1 tablespoon cornstarch
- 1 tablespoon of lemon juice

Topping:

- 1 cup rolled oatmeal
- 1/2 cup almond flour
- 1/4 cup honey
- 1/4 cup coconut oil, melted
- 1 teaspoon cinnamon
- Salt, a pinch

Instructions:

- Preheat your oven to 350°F (175°C).
- Rinse the mixed berries with water and dry them using a paper towel. Mix the berries in honey, cornstarch, and lemon juice.
- Spread the berry mixture in a baking dish.
- Mix the almond flour, honey, and coconut oil in a separate bowl until you have a crumbly mixture.
- Spread the topping evenly over the berries.
- Bake the mixed-berry crisp for 30 to 35 minutes, or until the topping turns golden brown and the berries start bubbling.
- Let the crisp cool down for a while before you serve it. Enjoy!

Peanut Butter Chocolate Chip Energy Bites

Peanut Butter Chocolate Chip Energy Bites can be a delicious and healthy snack that will satisfy your sweet tooth. These energy bites are high in fiber and protein, making them an excellent choice for mid-day snacking or pre-workout snacks.

Ingredients:

- 1 cup of old-fashioned oatmeal
- 1/2 cup peanut butter, creamy or crunchy
- 1/4 cup honey
- 1/4 cup dark chocolate chips
- 1 tsp vanilla extract
- 1/2 teaspoon cinnamon
- Salt pinch (optional).

Instructions:

- Combine the peanut butter, honey, and vanilla extract in a large bowl. Add salt if necessary.
- Mix until all ingredients are evenly combined
- Add the dark chocolate chips.
- Roll the mixture with your hands into small balls about 1 inch in diameter.
- To firm up, place the energy bites onto a parchment-lined baking sheet and freeze for 10-15 minutes.
- Once the energy bites are firm, transfer them to an airtight container. You can store the container in the refrigerator for up to one week.

Watermelon Popsicles

Watermelon popsicles are refreshing and healthy summer treats. These popsicles contain fresh watermelon and a little honey. There is no fat or salt added. Here is a recipe to make watermelon popsicles at your home.

Ingredients:

- 4 cups cubed seedless watermelon
- 2 tbsp honey
- 1 tbsp freshly squeezed lime juice
- 1/4 tsp salt (optional)

Instructions:

- Blend the watermelon, honey, and lime juice until smooth.
- Put the mixture in popsicle molds. Leave a little room at the top to allow expansion.
- Place popsicle sticks in the middle of each mold.
- Allow the popsicles to freeze for at least four hours or until solid.
- Run the molds under warm water for several seconds to remove the popsicles. Then, gently lift the popsicles from the molds.
- Enjoy your Watermelon Popsicles immediately!

CONCLUSION

In conclusion, making healthy choices in our daily diets is crucial for maintaining a healthy heart. With the Heart Healthy Cookbook for Beginners 2023 Edition, we hope to have provided you with a comprehensive guide to adopting a heart-healthy diet. Our book offers a wide range of low-sodium, low-fat recipes that are delicious and beneficial for your heart health.

We have discussed the basic principles of a heart-healthy diet, the benefits of such a diet, and the types of foods to eat, limit and avoid. We have also included a 30-day meal plan with breakfast, lunch, dinner, and dessert recipes. Our cookbook also includes vegetarian main course recipes, making it an excellent choice for vegetarians and non-vegetarians.

We believe that cooking should be an enjoyable experience, and we have tried our best to provide easy-to-follow recipes that even beginners can cook. To make it easier for you, we have included a cooking conversion chart that will help you convert ingredients and measurements to make your cooking experience stress-free.

In summary, we hope this cookbook will help you make informed choices about your diet and inspire you to cook delicious and heart-healthy meals for yourself and your loved ones. Remember, taking care of your heart starts with what you eat. With the Heart Healthy Cookbook for Beginners 2023 Edition, you can make healthy choices that will benefit your heart and overall well-being.

30 DAY MEAL PLAN

DAY	BREAKFAST	LUNCH	DINNER
Day 1	Sweet Potato and Spinach Hash	Cauliflower and chickpea salad	Grilled chicken with vegetable and chickpea stew
Day 2	Oatmeal with Berries and Almond Milk	Carrot and ginger soup	Broiled scallops with roasted root vegetables
Day 3	Peanut Butter Banana Toast	Ginger Tofu and vegetable kebabs	Baked tofu with sautéed kale and mushrooms
Day 4	Avocado Toast and Egg	Spinach and feta omelette	Grilled chicken with vegetable and quinoa salad
Day 5	Quinoa Breakfast Bowl	Red pepper and eggplant sandwich	Baked salmon and roasted asparagus with quinoa
Day 6	Greek Yoghurt with fruit and nuts	Brown rice and vegetable bowl	Grilled shrimp and mixed vegetables
Day 7	Healthy Breakfast Burrito	Grilled chicken and veggie salad with balsamic dressing	Lentil vegetable stir fry over brown rice
Day 8	Heart-healthy breakfast smoothie	Baked salmon and asparagus	Baked chicken with vegetable casserole
Day 9	Veggie Omelette	Shrimp and vegetable stew	Grilled steak with roasted peppers and onions
Day 10	Whole grain pancakes with fruit	Grilled vegetable and feta wrap	Slow-cooker vegetable soup
Day 11	Oatmeal with berries and almond milk	Lentil soup with spinach	Baked eggplant with tomatoes and mozzarella cheese
Day 12	Avocado toast and egg	Broccoli, and cheddar soup	Curry with shrimps and vegetables over brown rice
Day 13	Greek yoghurt with fruit and nuts	Sweet potato chili	Grilled chicken and vegetable kebabs
Day 14	Hearth-healthy breakfast smoothie	Grilled Portobello mushroom sandwich	Baked turkey meatballs and zucchini noodles
Day 15	Wholegrain pancakes with fruits	Goat cheese and roasted red pepper sandwich	Broiled cod with roasted Brussel sprouts

Day 16	Healthy breakfast burrito	Whole wheat pita with hummus and veggies	Tuna salad with avocado and mixed greens
Day 17	Quinoa breakfast	Chickpea salad with lemon and parsley	Sweet potato fried and grilled turkey burgers
Day 18	Peanut butter banana toast	Grilled chicken and veggie skewers	Grilled shrimp and pineapple skewers.
Day 19	Sweet potato toast	Black bean vegetable quesadilla	Vegetable lentil curry over brown rice.
Day 20	Greek yoghurt with fruit and nuts	Smoked salmon sandwich	Baked salmon with steamed green beans and quinoa
Day 21	Avocado toast and egg	Vegetable wrap and Greek yoghurt	Grilled pork tenderloin and roasted root vegetables
Day 22	Veggie omelette	Tuna Salad lettuce wraps	Quinoa and vegetable-stuffed bell peppers
Day 23	Peanut butter banana toast	Quinoa, lentil salad with roasted vegetables	Sweet potato and baked chicken
Day 24	Whole grain pancakes with fruits	Grilled chicken salad with veggies	Spicy lentil soup with whole wheat bread
Day 25	Oatmeal with berries and almond milk	Sandwich with turkey and avocado	Stir-fried chicken with vegetables and brown rice
Day 26	Veggie omelette	Goat cheese and roasted red pepper sandwich	Sweet potato baked with steamed spinach and chickpeas
Day 27	Heart-healthy breakfast smoothie	Grilled vegetable and feta wrap	Grilled shrimps and vegetable kebobs
Day 28	Sweet potato and spinach hash	Baked salmon and asparagus	Steamed asparagus and broiled salmon with quinoa
Day 29	Greek yoghurt with fruit and nuts	Carrot and ginger soup	Grilled chicken and roasted vegetables
Day 30	Veggie omelette	Sweet Potato chili	Slow-cooker vegetable soup

BASIC CONVERSION CHARTS

weight
(rounded to the nearest whole number)

IMPERIAL	METRIC
0.5 oz	14 g
1 oz	28 g
2 oz	58 g
3 oz	86 g
4 oz	114 g
5 oz	142 g
6 oz	170 g
7 oz	198 g
8 oz (1/2 lb)	226 g
9 oz	256 g
10 oz	284 g
11 oz	312 g
12 oz	340 g
13 oz	368 g
14 oz	396 g
15 oz	426 g
16 oz (1 lb)	454 g
24 oz (1 1/2 lb)	680 g

misc
(rounded to the closest equivalent)

IMPERIAL	
1 quart	4 cups (1 liter)
4 quarts	16 cups (4.5 liters)
6 quarts	24 cups (7 liters)
1 gallon	16 cups (4.5 liters)

volume
(rounded to the closest equivalent)

IMPERIAL	METRIC
1/8 tsp	0.5 mL
1/4 tsp	1 mL
1/2 tsp	2.5 mL
3/4 tsp	4 mL
1 tsp	5 mL
1 tbsp	15 mL
1 1/2 tbsp	25 mL
1/8 cup	30 mL
1/4 cup	60 mL
1/3 cup	80 mL
1/2 cup	120 mL
2/3 cup	160 mL
3/4 cup	180 mL
1 cup	240 mL

liquid
(rounded to the closest equivalent)

IMPERIAL	METRIC
0.5 oz	15 mL
1 oz	30 mL
2 oz	60 mL
3 oz	85 mL
4 oz	115 mL
5 oz	140 mL
6 oz	170 mL
7 oz	200 mL
8 oz	230 mL
9 oz	260 mL
10 oz	285 mL
11 oz	310 mL
12 oz	340 mL
13 oz	370 mL

temperature
(rounded to the closest equivalent)

IMPERIAL	METRIC
150°F	65°C
160°F	70°C
175°F	80°C
200°F	95°C
225°F	110°C
250°F	120°C
275°F	135°C
300°F	150°C
325°F	160°C
350°F	175°C
375°F	190°C
400°F	205°C
425°F	220°C
450°F	230°C
475°F	245°C
500°F	260°C

length
(rounded to the closest equivalent)

IMPERIAL	METRIC
1/8 inch	3 mm
1/4 inch	6 mm
1 inch	2.5 cm
1 1/4 inch	3 cm
2 inches	5 cm
6 inches	15 cm
8 inches	20 cm
9 inches	22.5 cm
10 inches	25 cm
11 inches	28 cm

COOKING MEASUREMENT CONVERSION CHART

QUICK ALTERNATIVES

1 tablespoon (tbsp)	3 teaspoons (tsp)
1/16 cup	1 tablespoon
1/8 cup	2 tablespoons
1/6 cup	2 tablespoons + 2 teaspoons
1/4 cup	4 tablespoons
1/3 cup	5 tablespoons + 1 teaspoon
3/8 cup	6 tablespoons
1/2 cup	8 tablespoons
2/3 cup	10 tablespoons + 2 teaspoons
3/4 cup	12 tablespoons
1 cup	48 teaspoons
1 cup	16 tablespoons
8 fluid ounces (fl oz)	1 cup
1 pint (pt)	2 cups
1 quart (qt)	2 pints
4 cups	1 quart
1 gallon (gal)	4 quarts
16 ounces (oz)	1 pound (lb)
1 milliliter (ml)	1 cubic centimeter (cc)
1 inch (in)	2.54 centimeters (cm)

CAPACITY (U.S to Metric)

1/5 teaspoon	1 milliliter
1 teaspoon	5 ml
1 tablespoon	15 ml
1 fluid oz	30 ml
1/5 cup	47 ml
1 cup	237 ml
2 cups (1 pint)	473 ml
4 cups (1 quart)	.95 liter
4 quarts (1 gal.)	3.8 liters

WEIGHT (U.S to Metric)

1 oz	28	grams
1 pound	454	grams

CAPACITY (Metric to U.S.)

1 milliliter	1/5	teaspoon
5 ml	1	teaspoon
15 ml	1	tablespoon
100 ml	3.4	fluid oz
240 ml	1	cup
	34	fluid oz
	4.2	cups
1 liter	2.1	pints
	1.06	quarts
	0.26	gallon

WEIGHT (Metric to U.S.)

1 gram	0.035	ounce
100 grams	3.5	ounces
500 grams	1.1	pounds
1 kilogram	2.205	pounds
	35	ounces

INDEX

Made in the USA
Monee, IL
16 May 2023

33821581R00070